We keep swimming, until we all reach home

Jillian Guyette

Daylight

Publisher: Michael Itkoff
Creative Director: Ursula Damm
Copy Editor: Gabrielle Fastman

ISBN: 978-1-954119-47-5

Printed by Ofset Yapimevi, Turkey

Daylight Books
E-mail: info@daylightbooks.org
Web: www.daylightbooks.org

Inheritance

To be born is the first miracle.
My mother says I was born
Unwilling to face the right direction.
My daughter arrives much easier.
I tell her: *I carried you*
And you will carry me.
And she says, Mommy,
Why do you cry so much?

There was never any question
Of my purpose. I stood at the door
And opened it. A continent of hope
Held in the logistics of time.

I touch my daughter's face
And know it as my own.

—Kate Baer

We Keep Swimming, Until We All Reach Home

In the 1980s, my mother met my father when she went to him for a psychic reading. That foundation, initiated by wonder, met with love, fraught with stress, and followed by heartbreak, temporarily wrapped itself up in 2001 with his death, resulting from complications of emphysema. He was sixty-three; I was eleven. There was an almost certain guarantee that a child stemming from such nuance might move through the world perceiving things a bit differently. The weight of that difference coming most clearly into focus for me after I gave birth to my daughter.

My body and mind have spent years balancing the practical with the magical. Guided in the faith and mystery of something unseen, all while doing my best to stay grounded in the reality of the here and now. Layne Redmond writes in her book *When the Drummers Were Women: A Spiritual History of Rhythm*:

> It is often said that the first sound we hear in the womb is our mother's heartbeat. Actually, the first sound to vibrate our newly developed hearing apparatus is the pulse of our mother's blood through her veins and arteries. We vibrate to that primordial rhythm even before we have ears to hear. Before we were conceived, we existed in part as an egg in our mother's ovary. All the eggs a woman will ever carry form in her ovaries while she is a four-month-old fetus in the womb of her mother. This means our cellular life as an egg begins in the womb of our grandmother. Each of us spent five months in our grandmother's womb

> and she in turn formed within the womb of her grandmother. We vibrate to the rhythms of our mother's blood before she herself is born. And this pulse is the thread of blood that runs all the way back through the grandmothers to the first mother. We all share the blood of the first mother. We are truly children of one blood.

When I was eight months pregnant with my daughter, an artist told me while she was offering me an energy reading that my daughter and I had done this before. While pregnancy was uncomfortable and motherhood a mystery, that much I could already feel. There are times now when she feels like my mother, like at some point in another life she was desperately trying to comb my hair, exhausted by the thought of sitting by my side until I wiggled my way to sleep, seething with frustration, overwhelmed with guilt, in utter awe of the magic of it all.

I look at my daughter and I see my mother. I see me. All of us, one by one, piece by piece. Quick and curious glimpses of inherited histories, inherited wounds. A familiar yet hazy hand-me-down of a memory. You can't quite place why, but there's a rhythm to it all. A privilege to the age and history that all of these mothers hold, spoken in a language I now understand with a different type of fluency. Anchored by my child, and shored by memory.

—Jillian Guyette

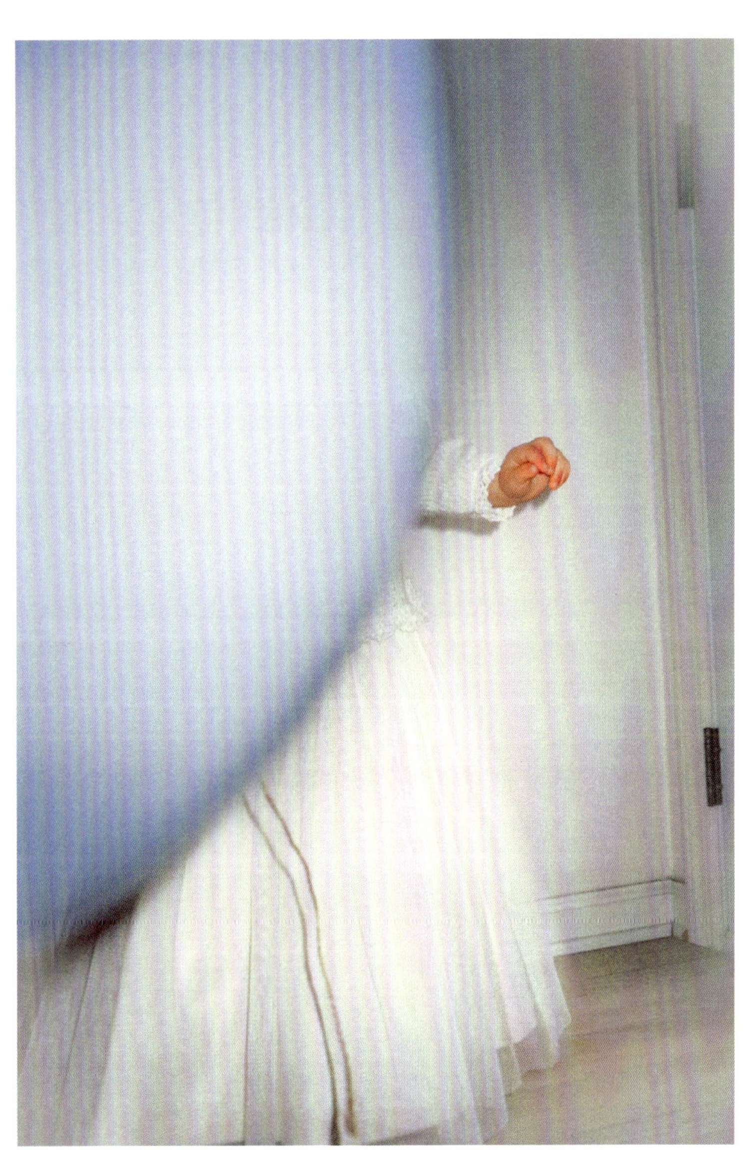

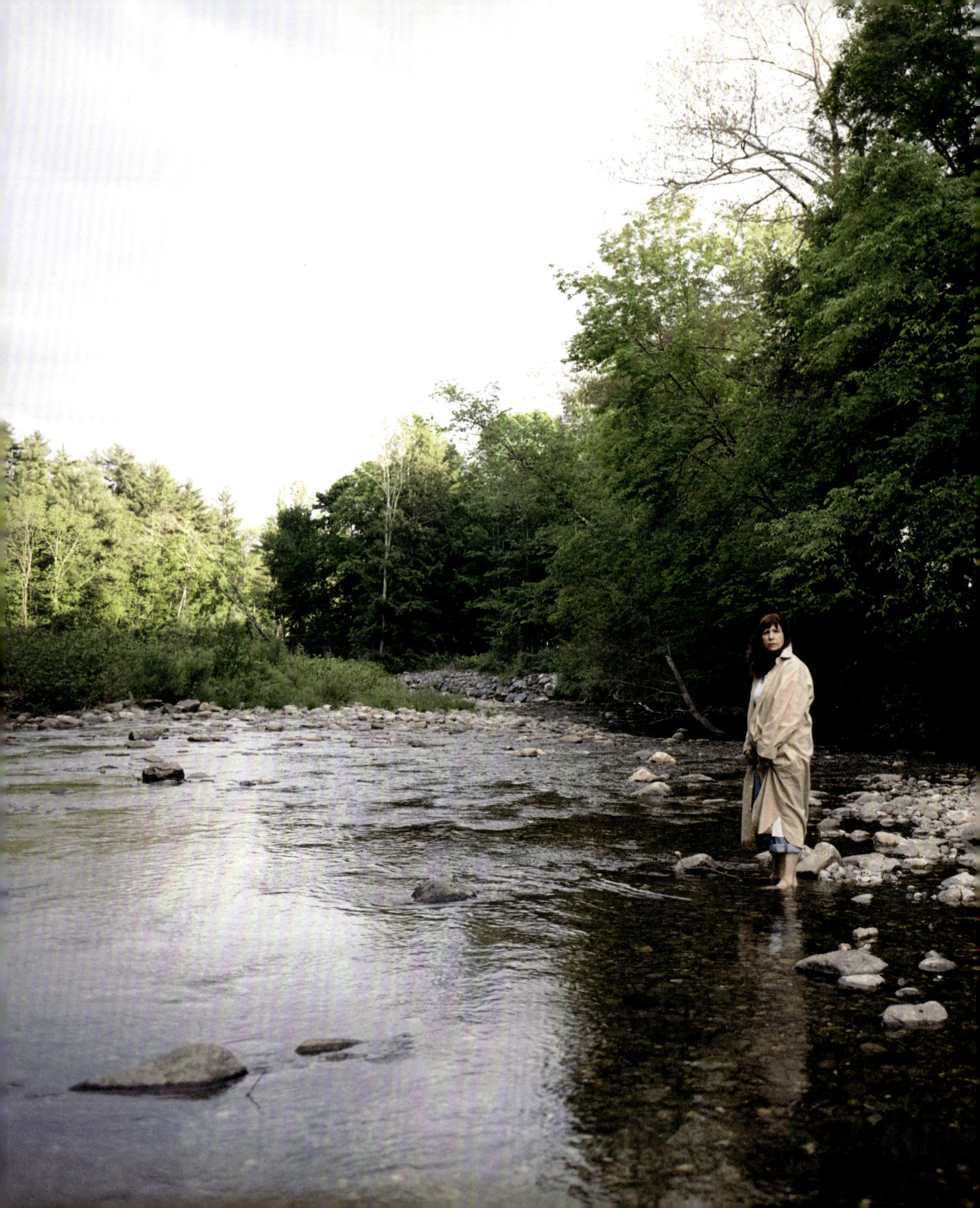

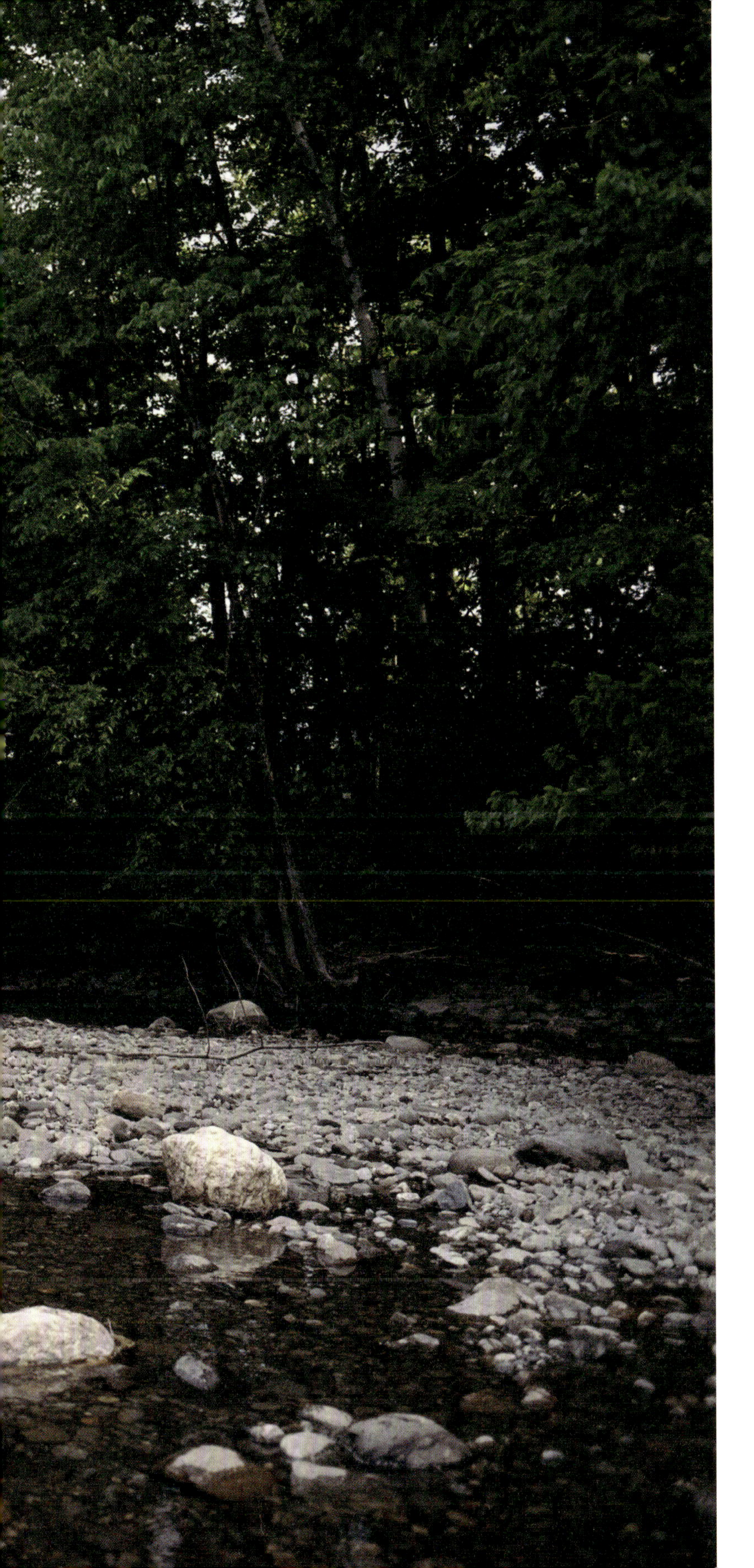

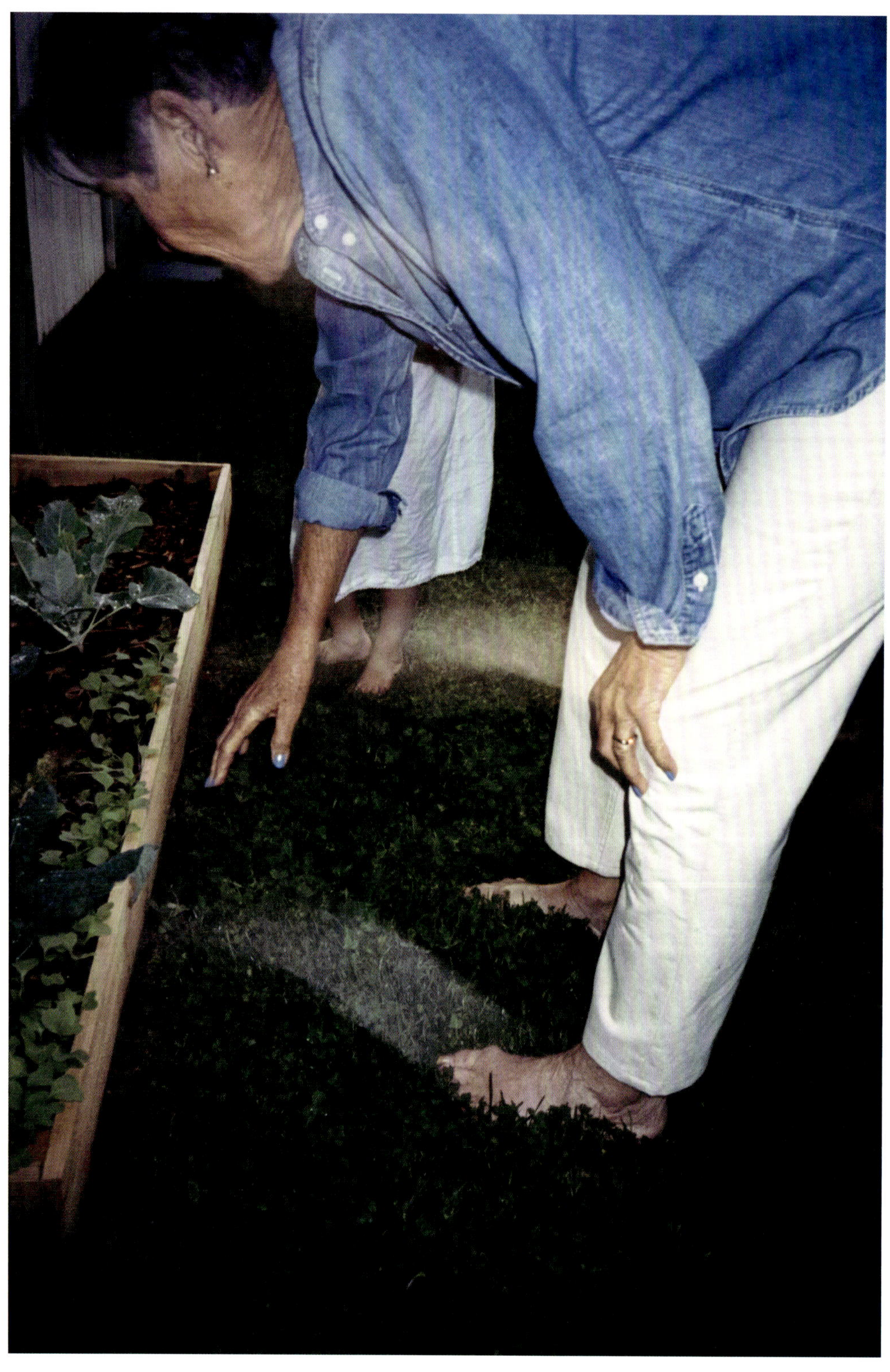

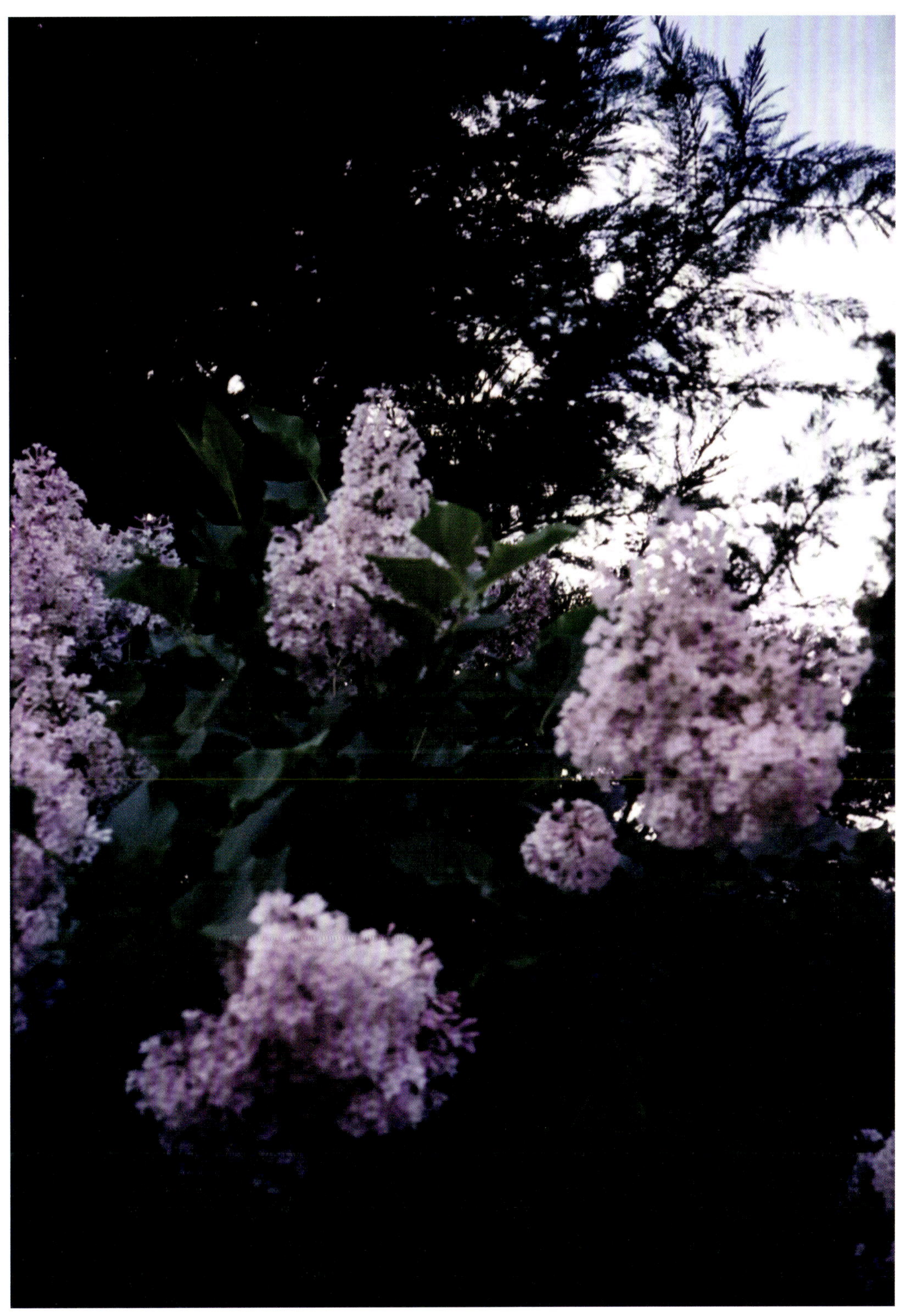

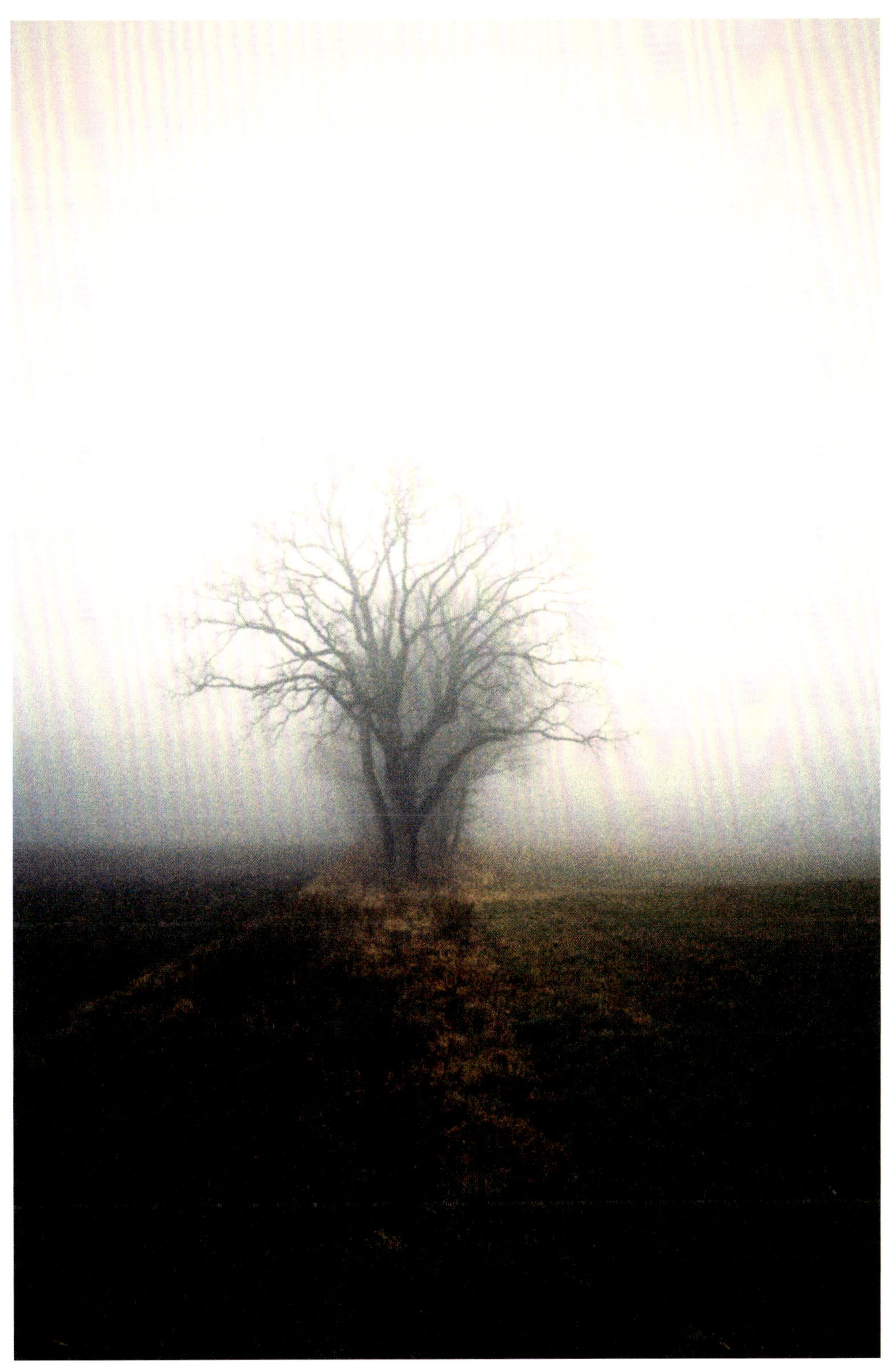

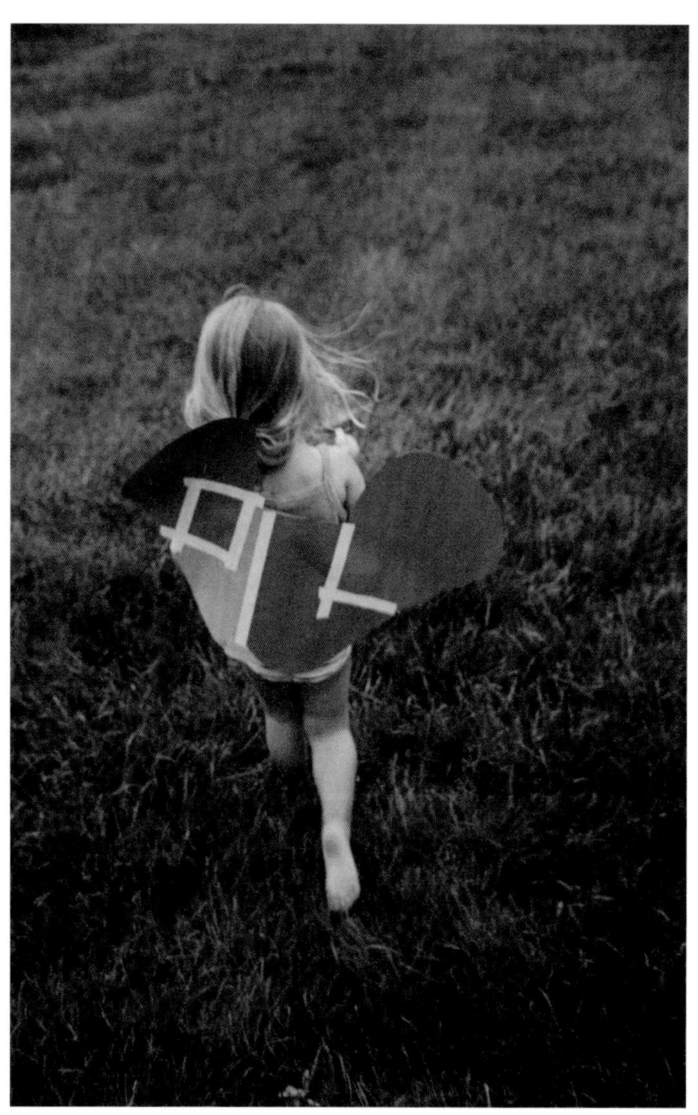

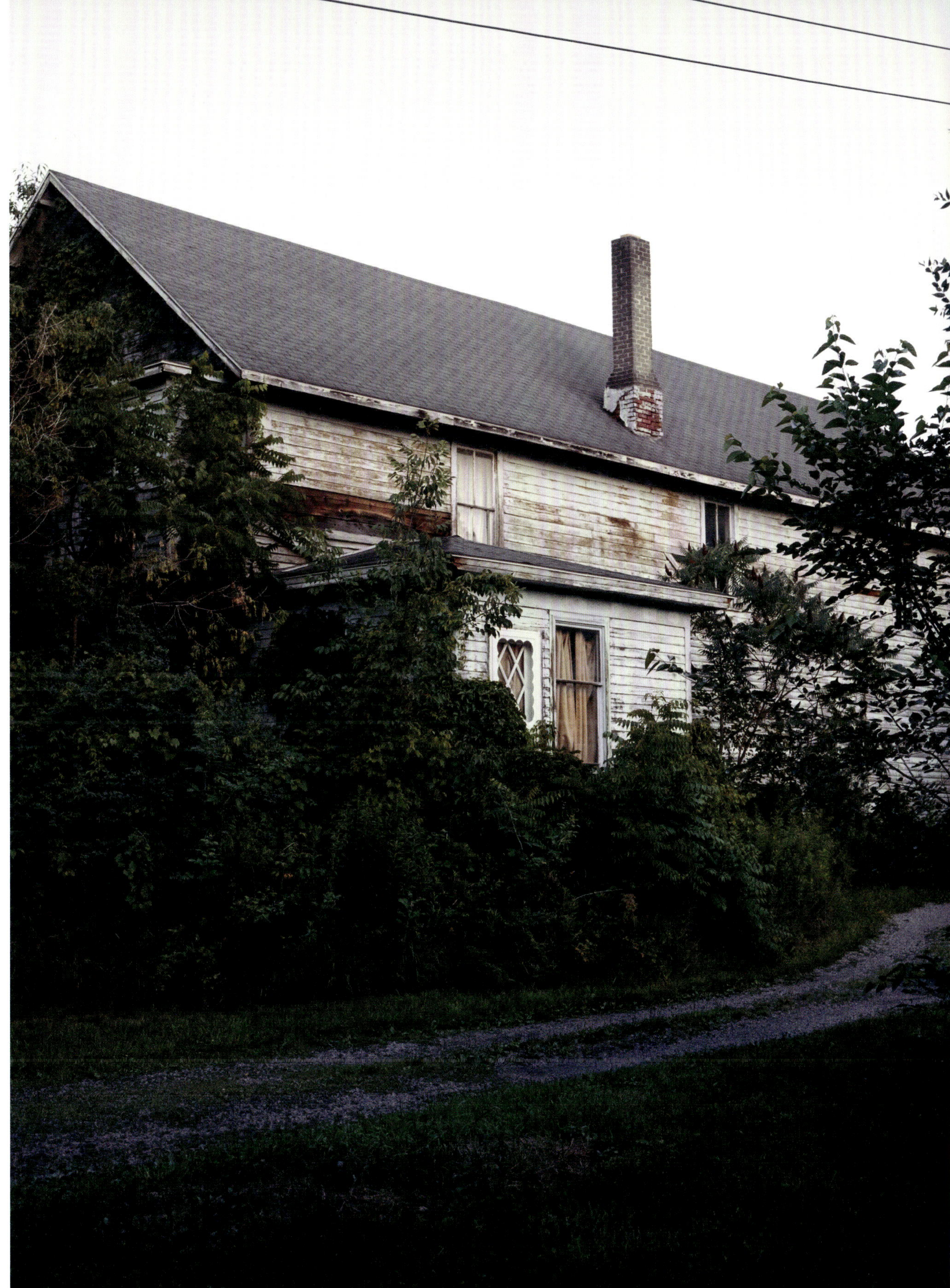

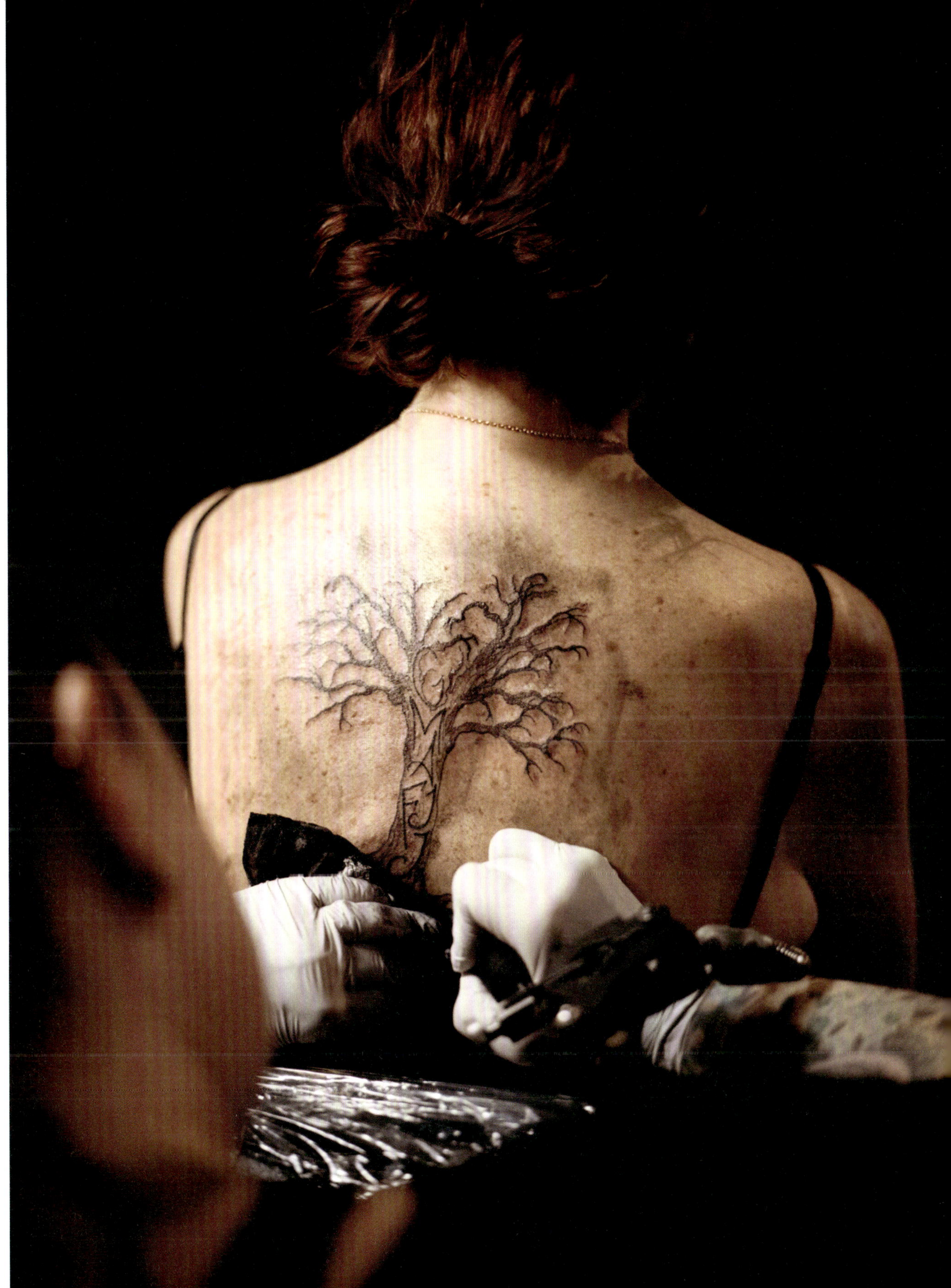

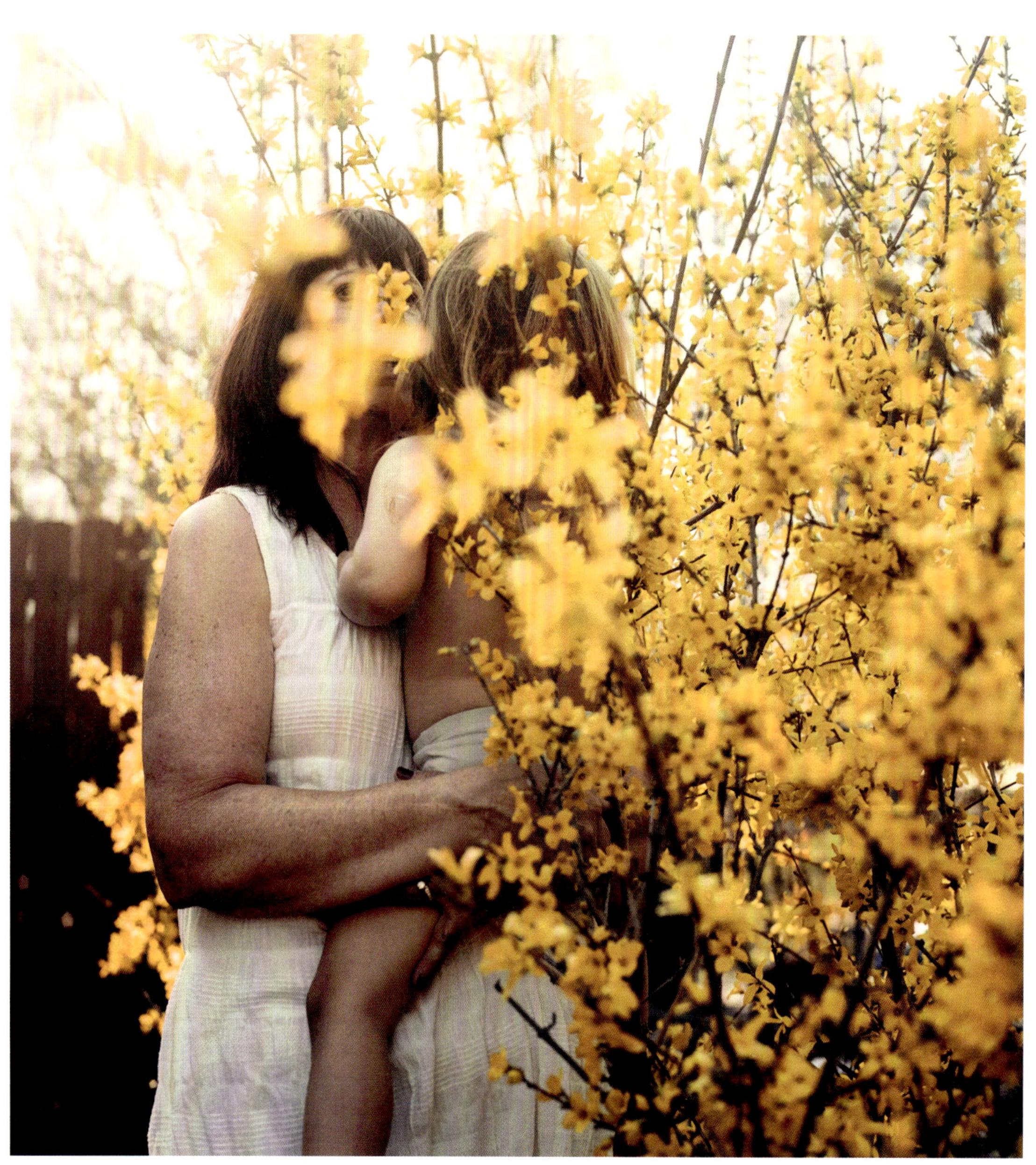

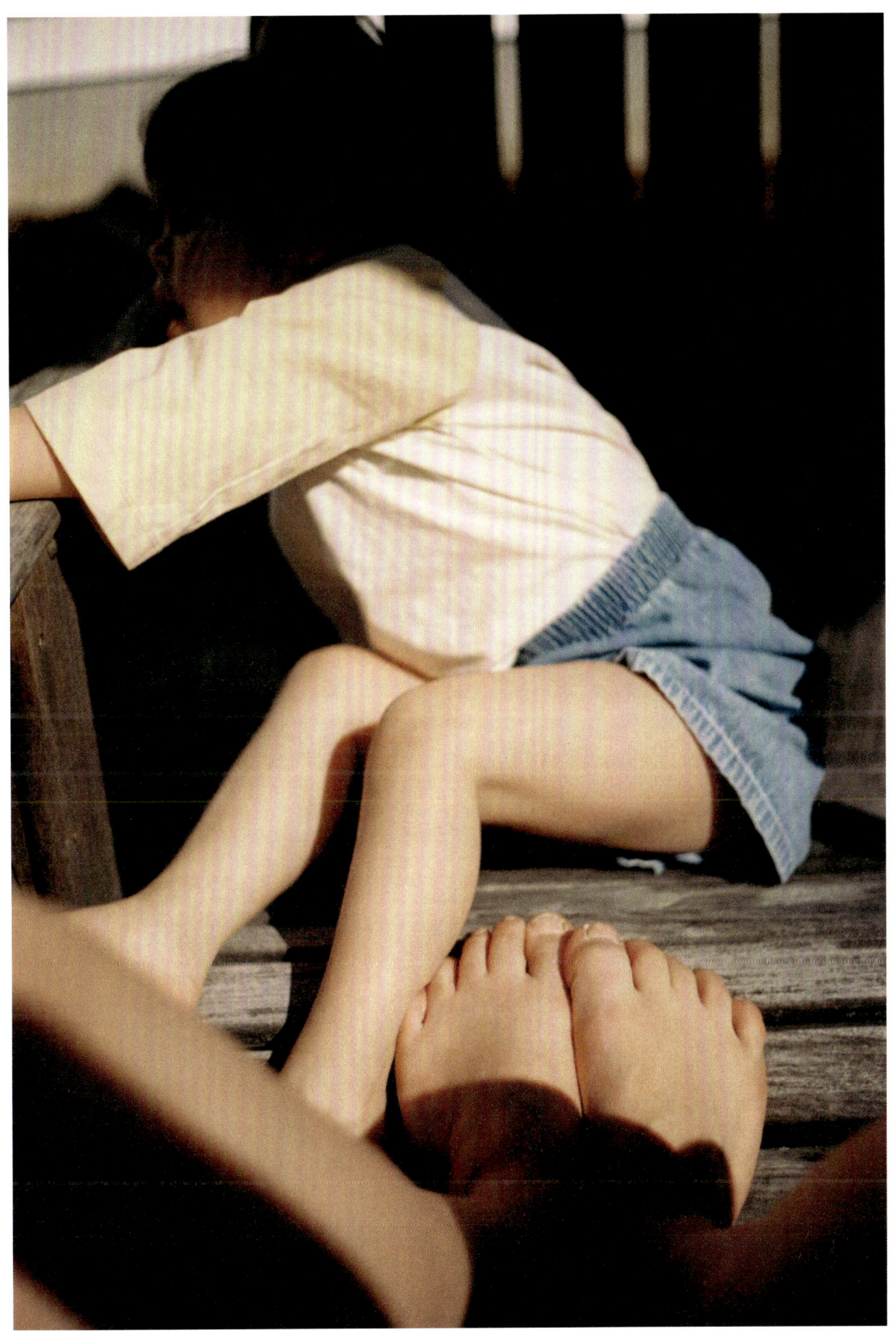

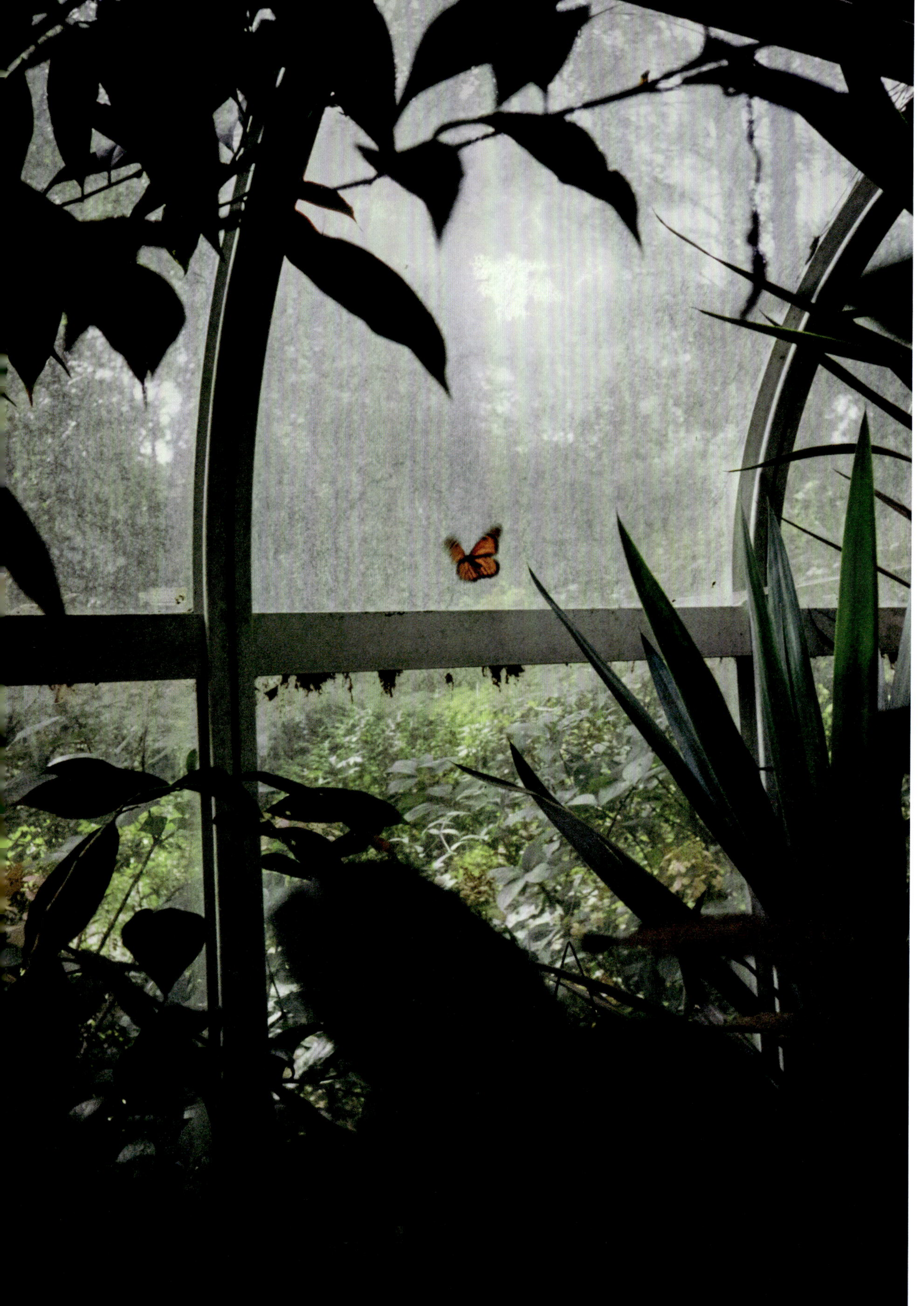

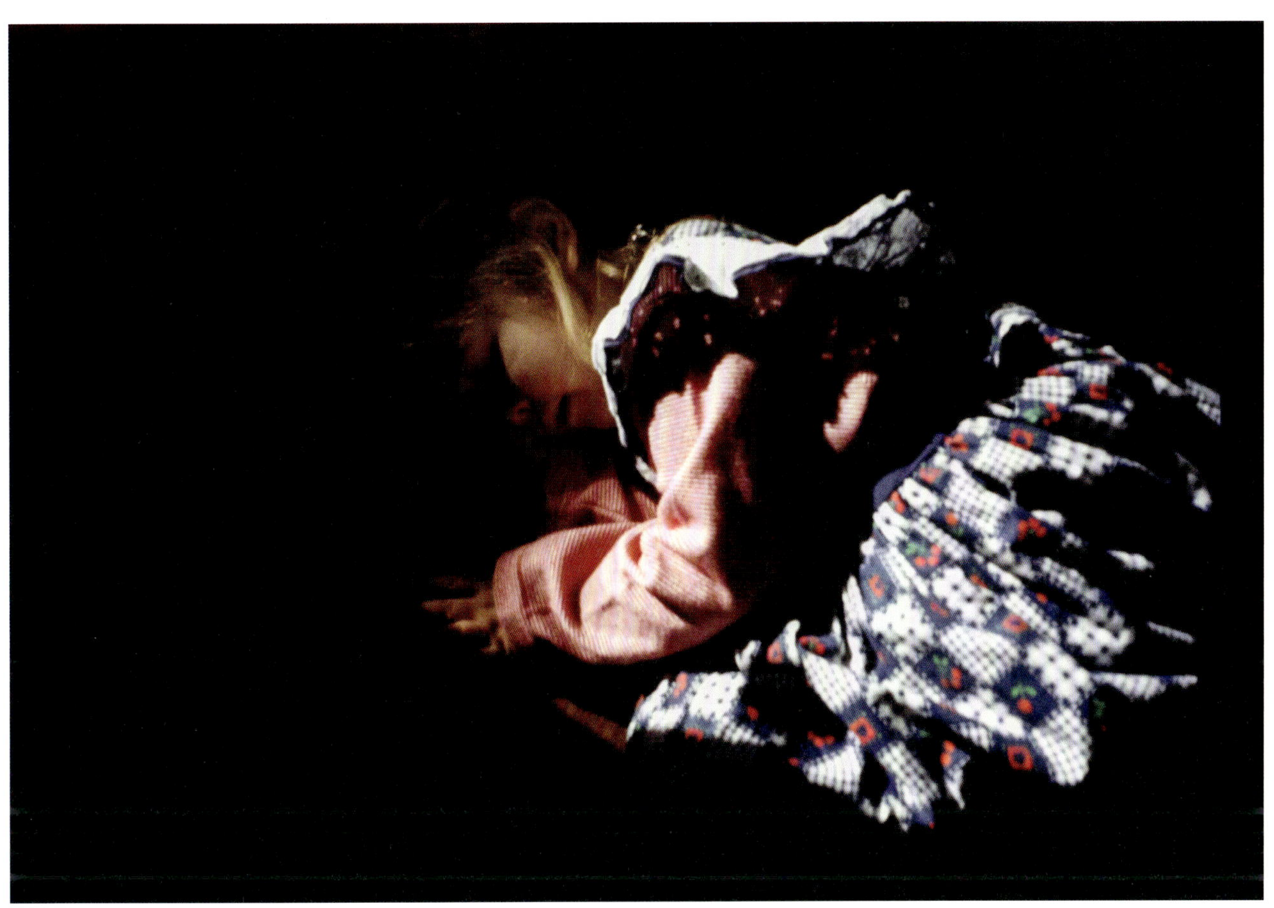

My daughter tells me about her other mommy sometimes, the one she had before me. Usually she talks about it during the pauses, the in-between. After I've read her a bedtime story, while she's singing along to Linger or Tom's Diner in the car.

It's a sunny afternoon when I pick her up from school and she pauses, as I buckle her into her car seat. "Mommy, you're a good mommy, but I miss my other mommy sometimes."

"That's okay to miss your other mommy, which mommy is this again?" I've learned that if I sound too interested she'll stop talking.

"The one I had before you and daddy were my parents. There was lots of blood. We were holding hands and then she was gone. But I was okay, and now I have you."

And now, I have you too.

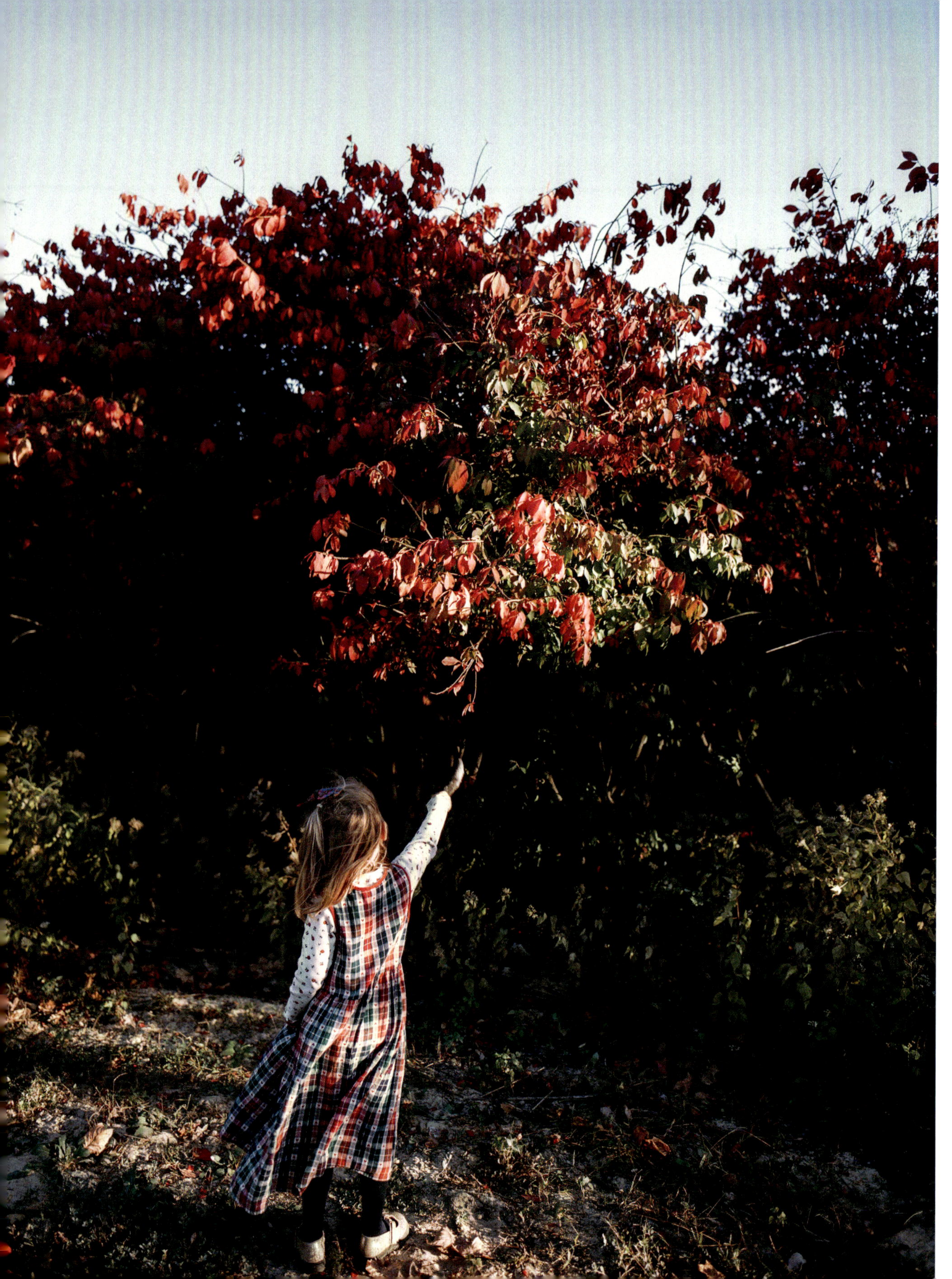

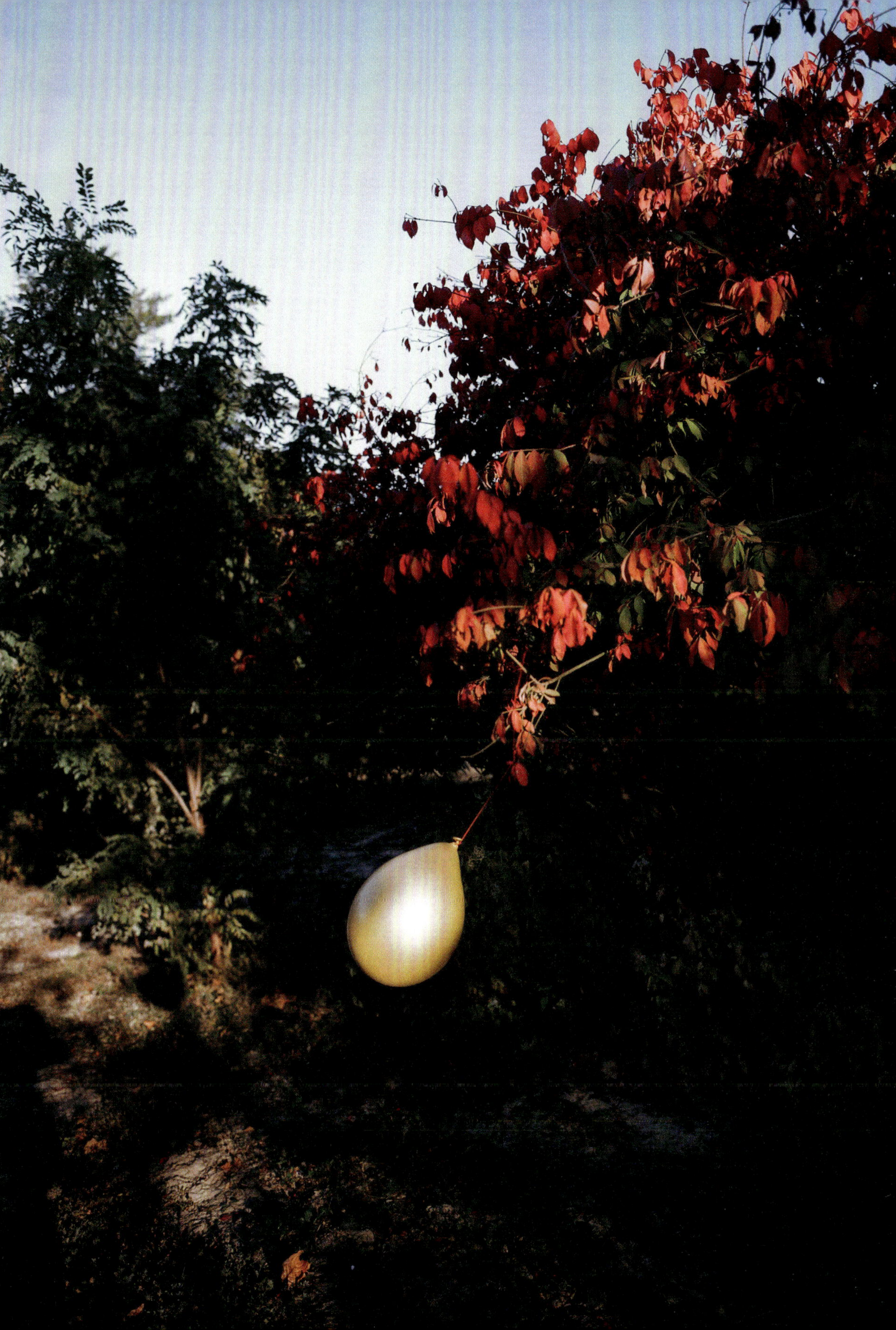

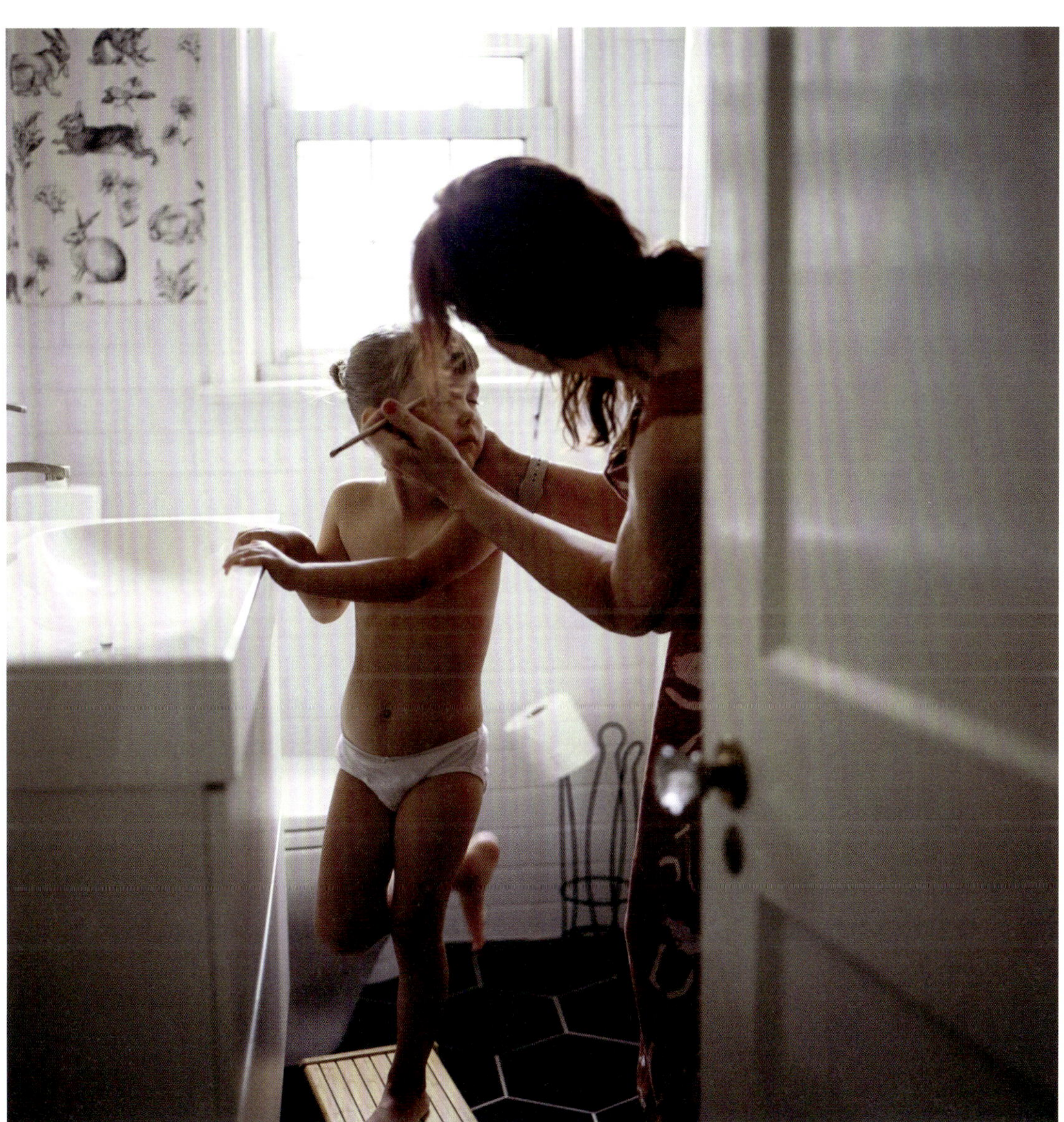

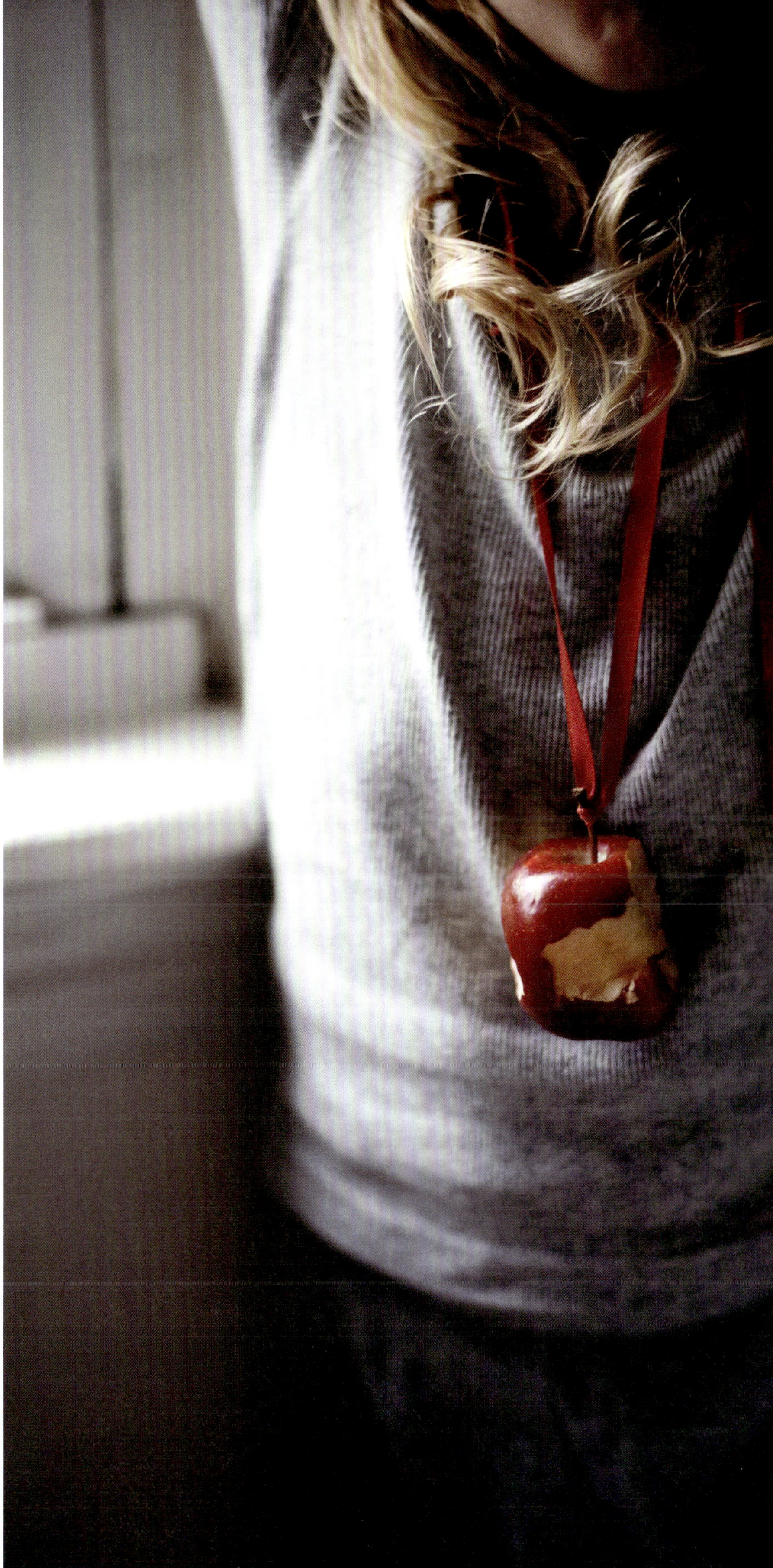

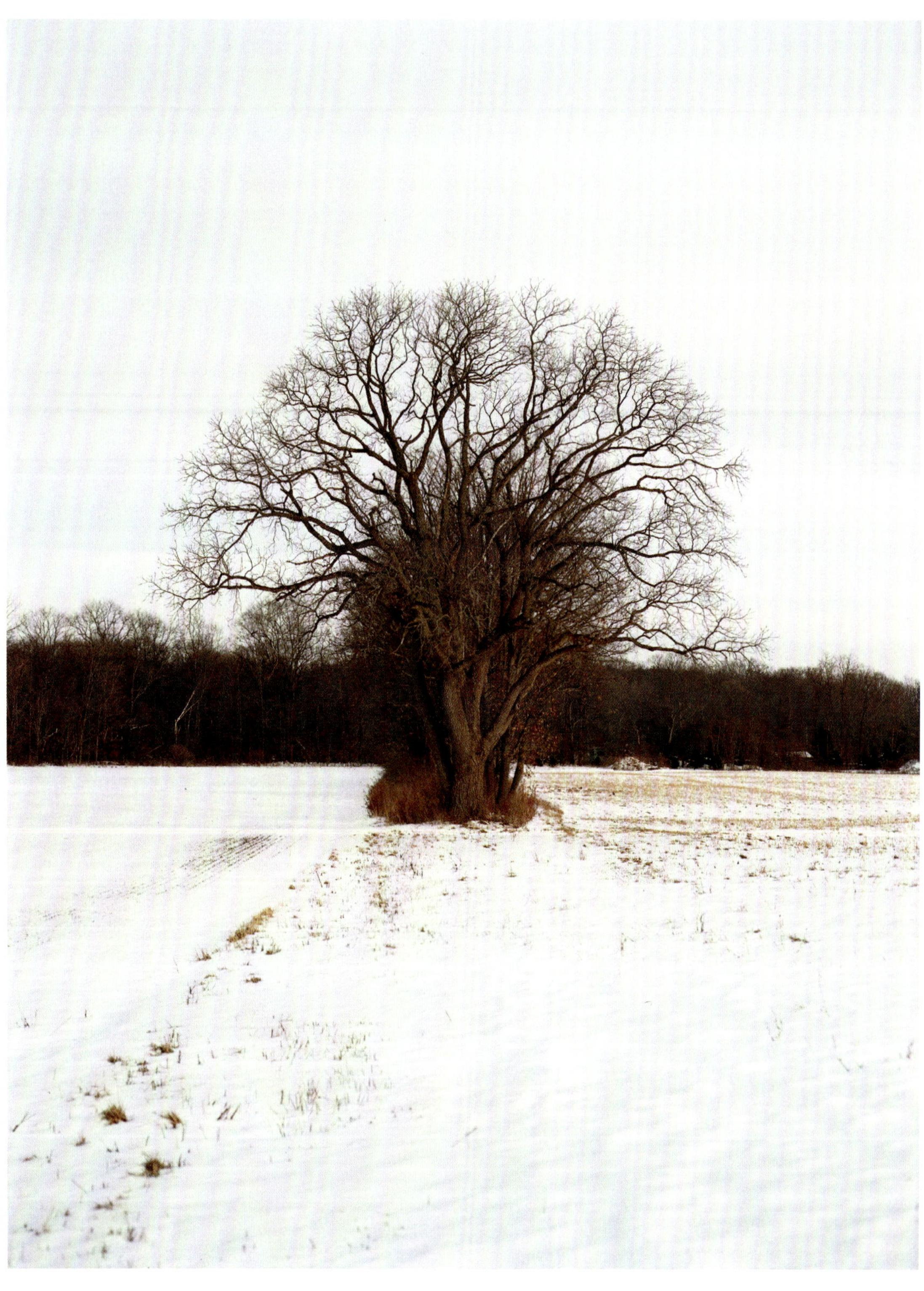

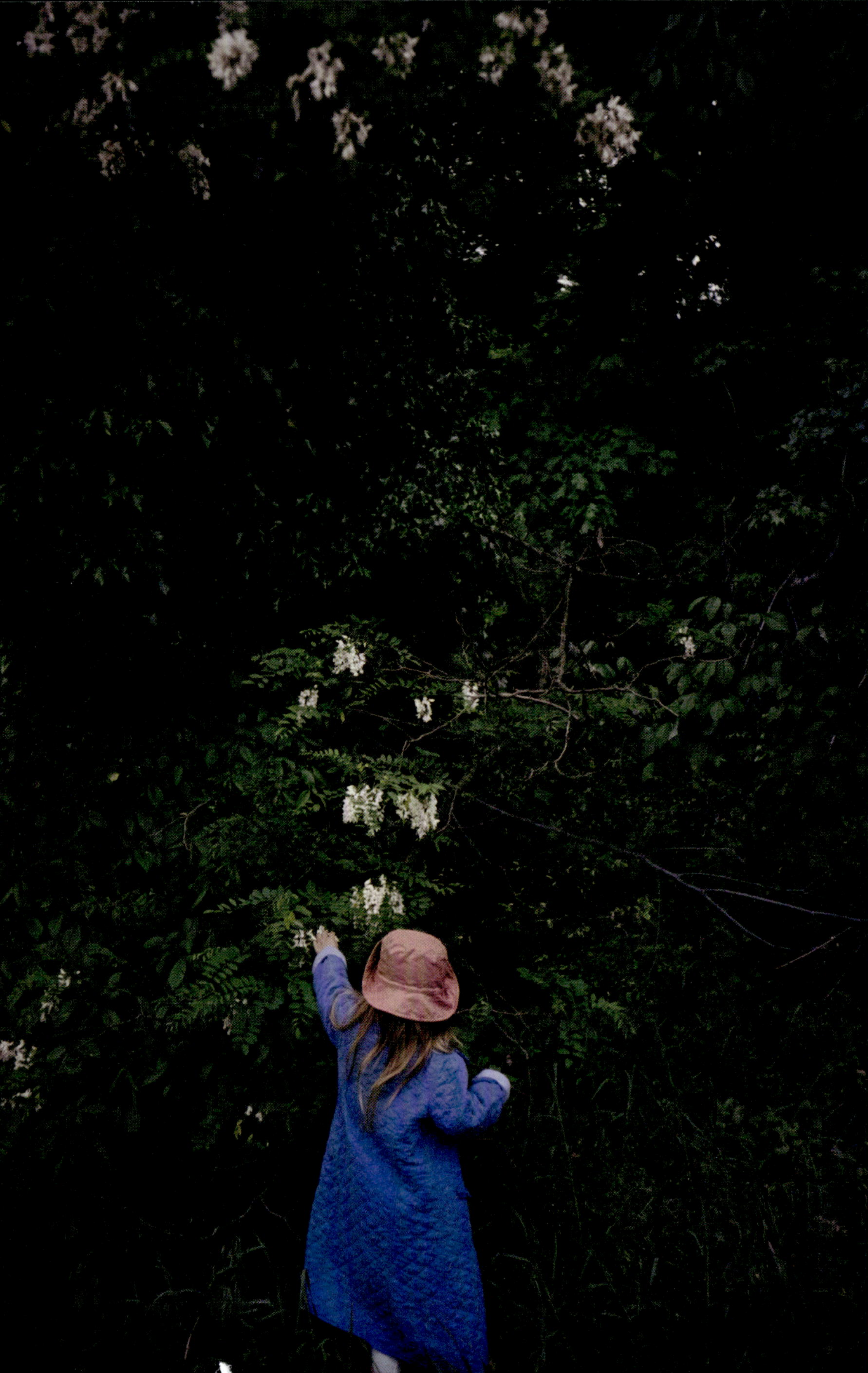

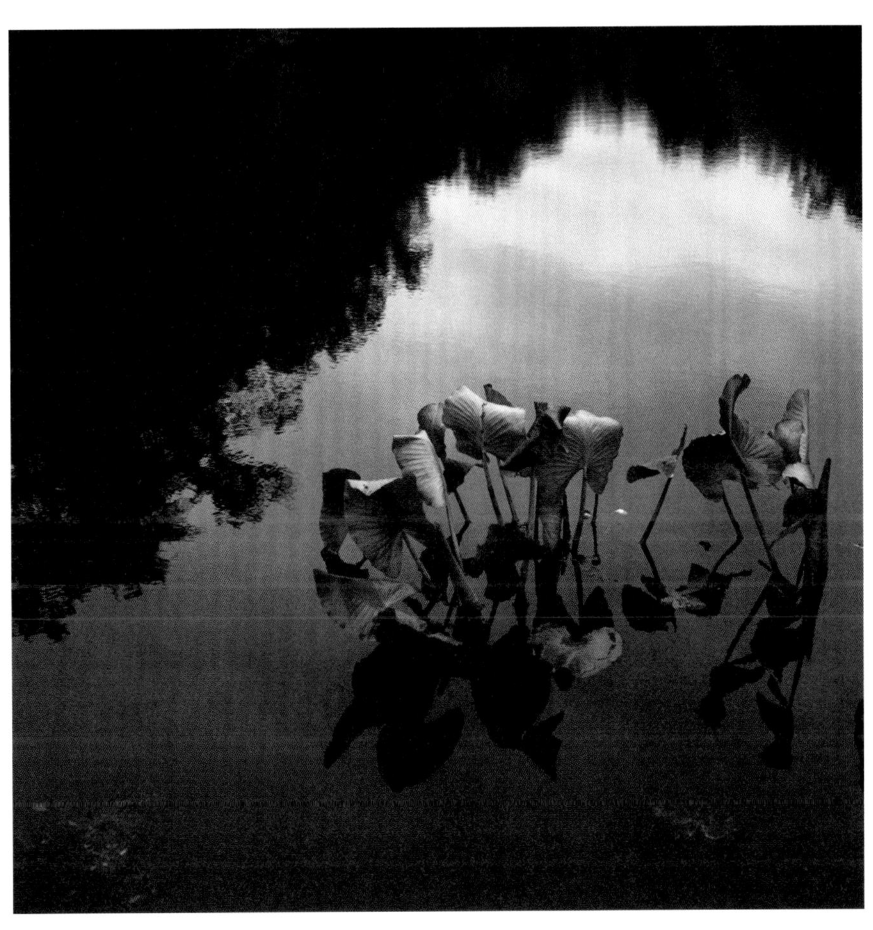

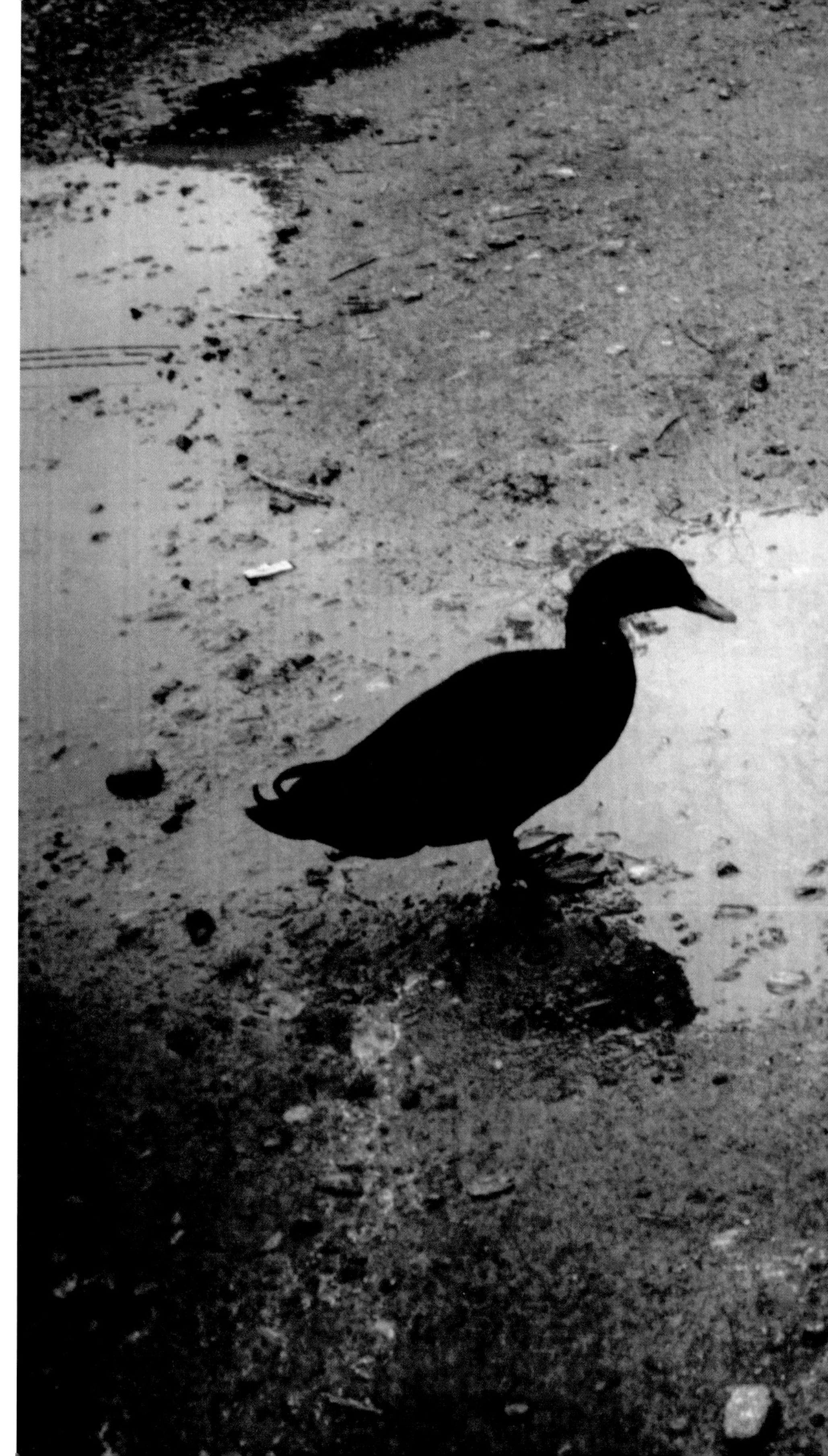

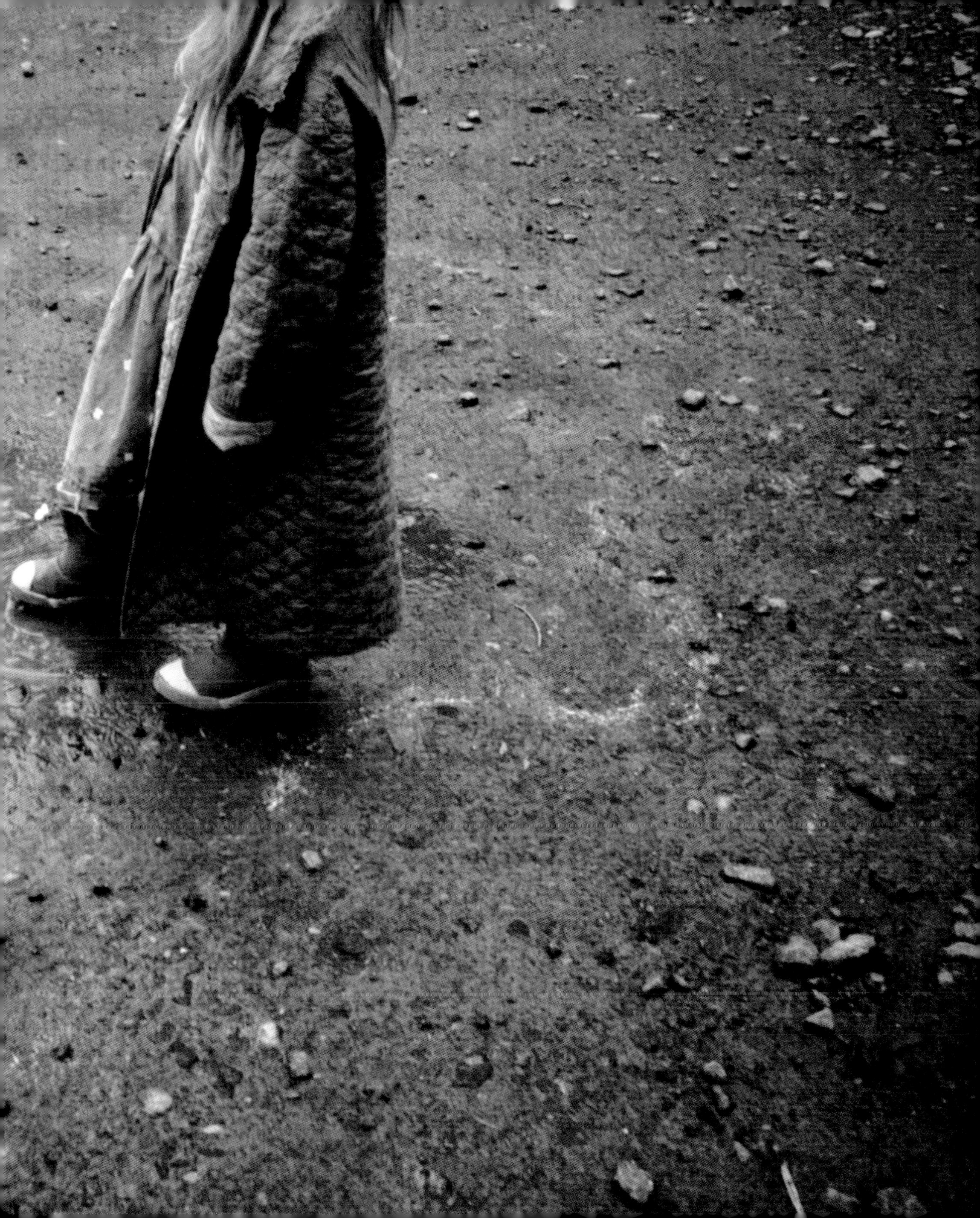

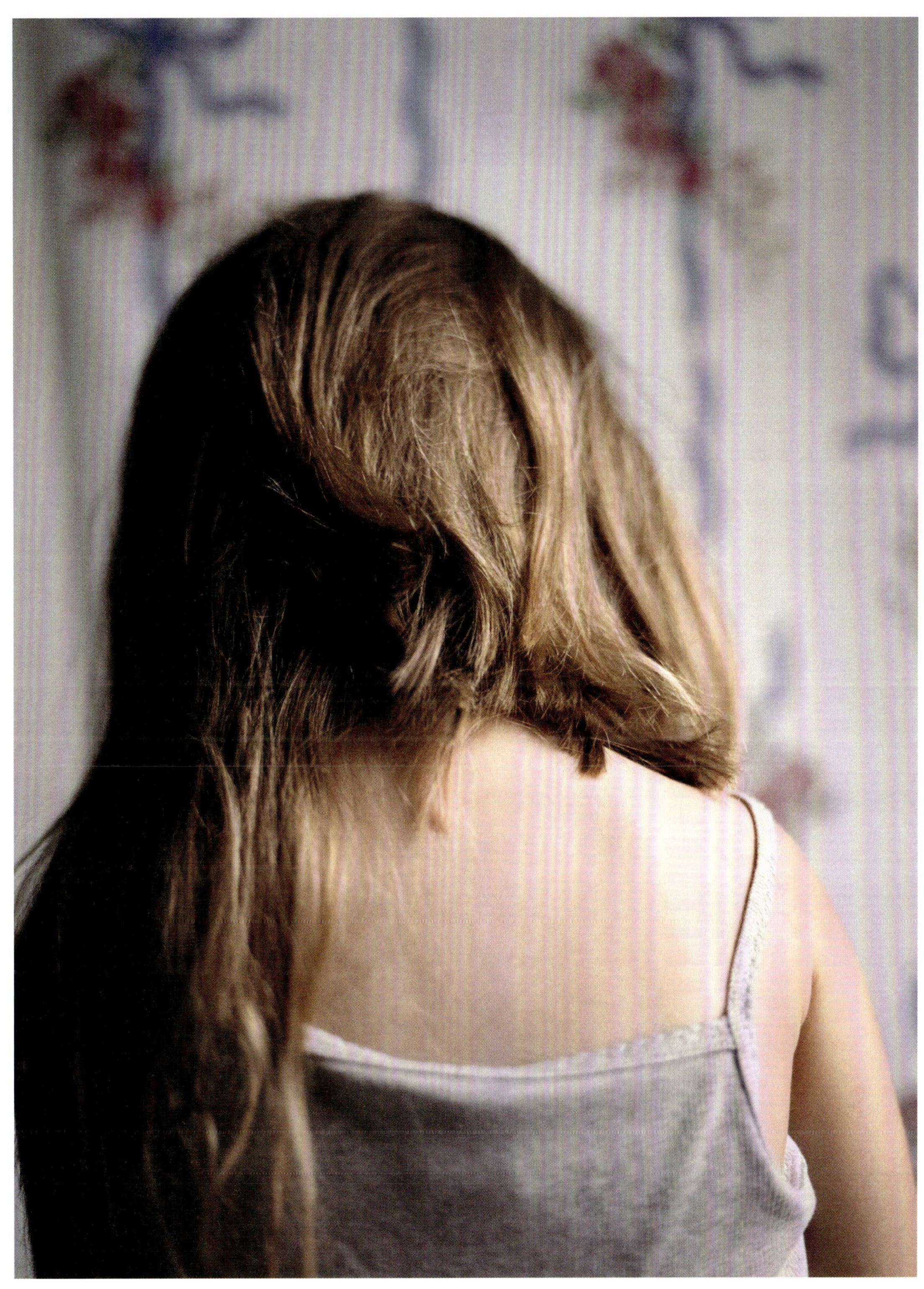

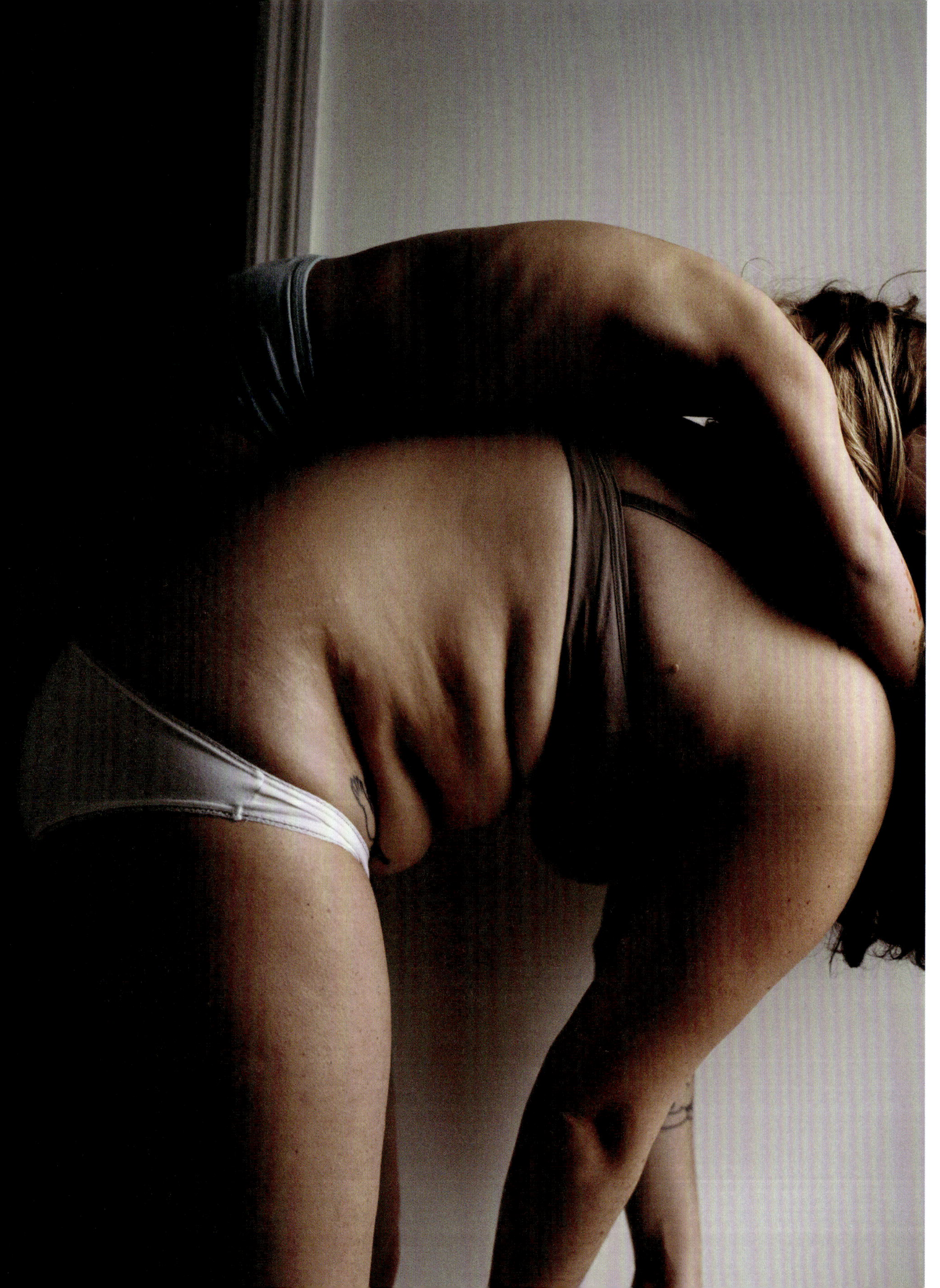

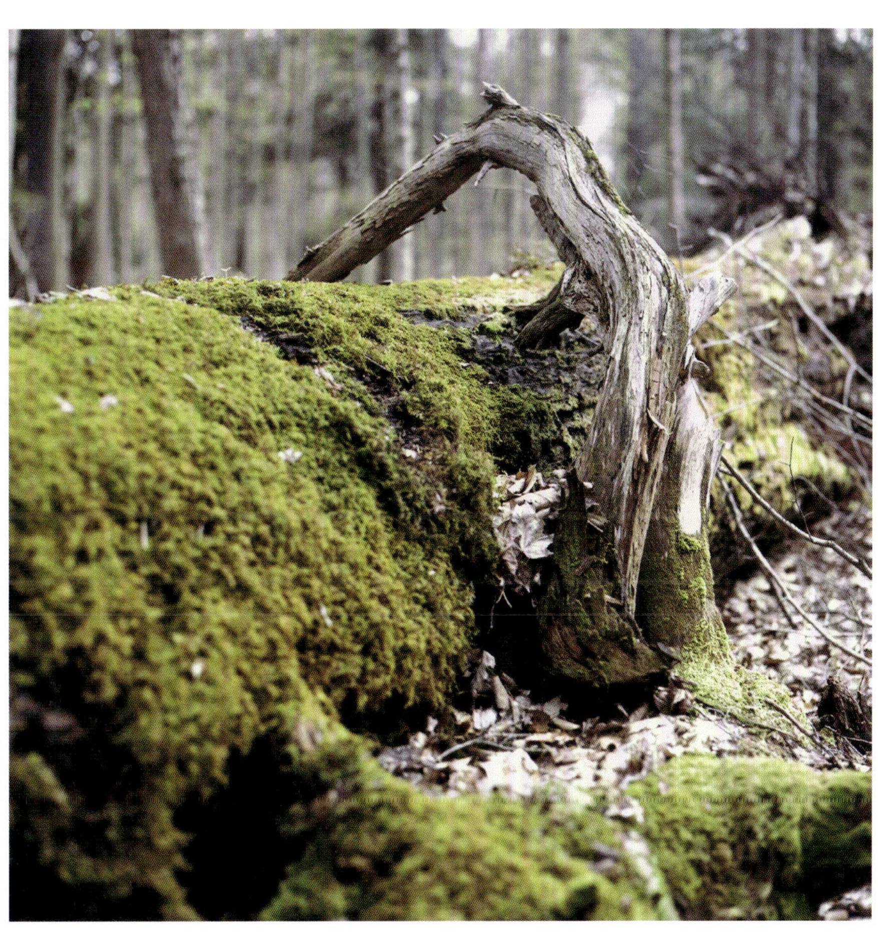

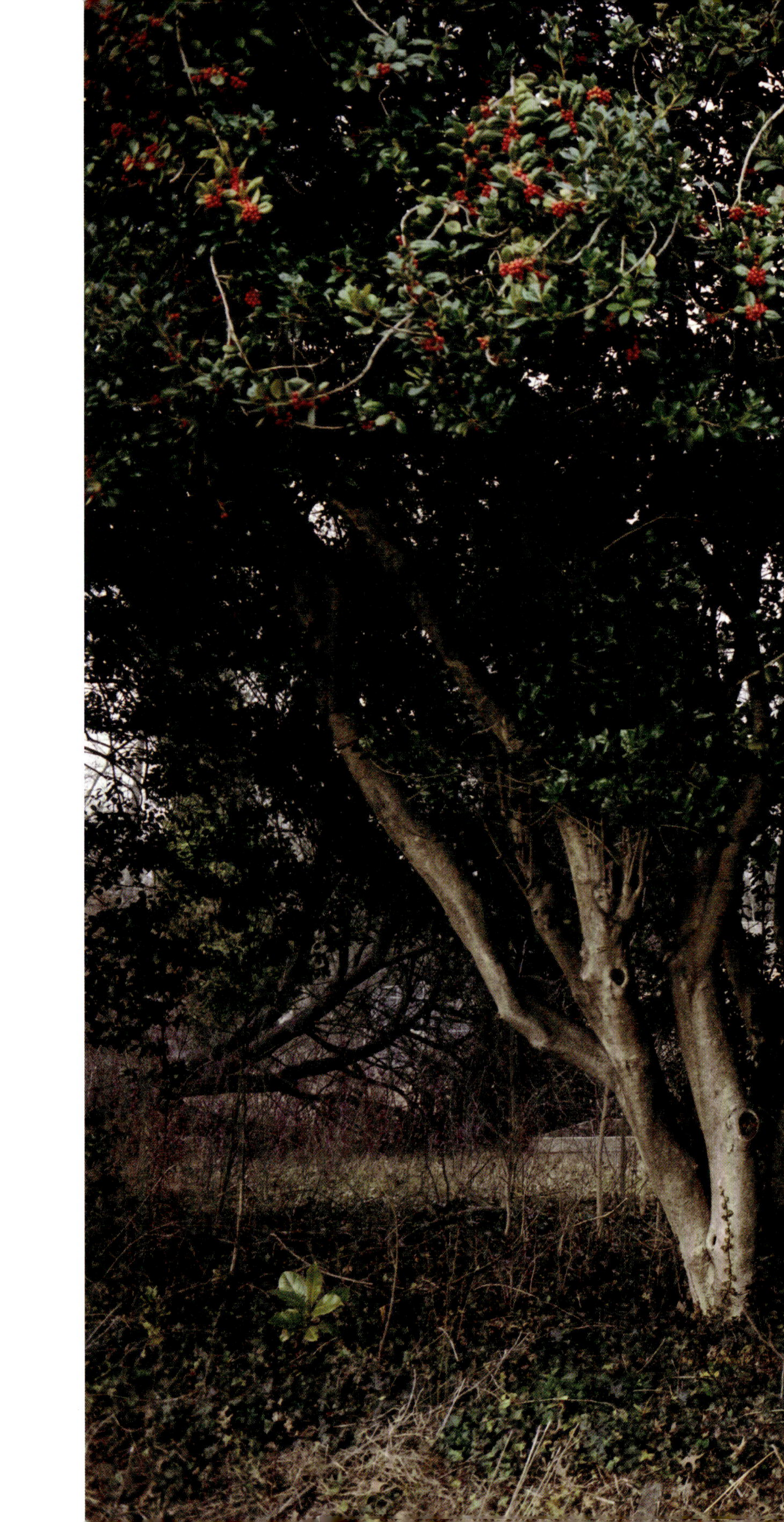

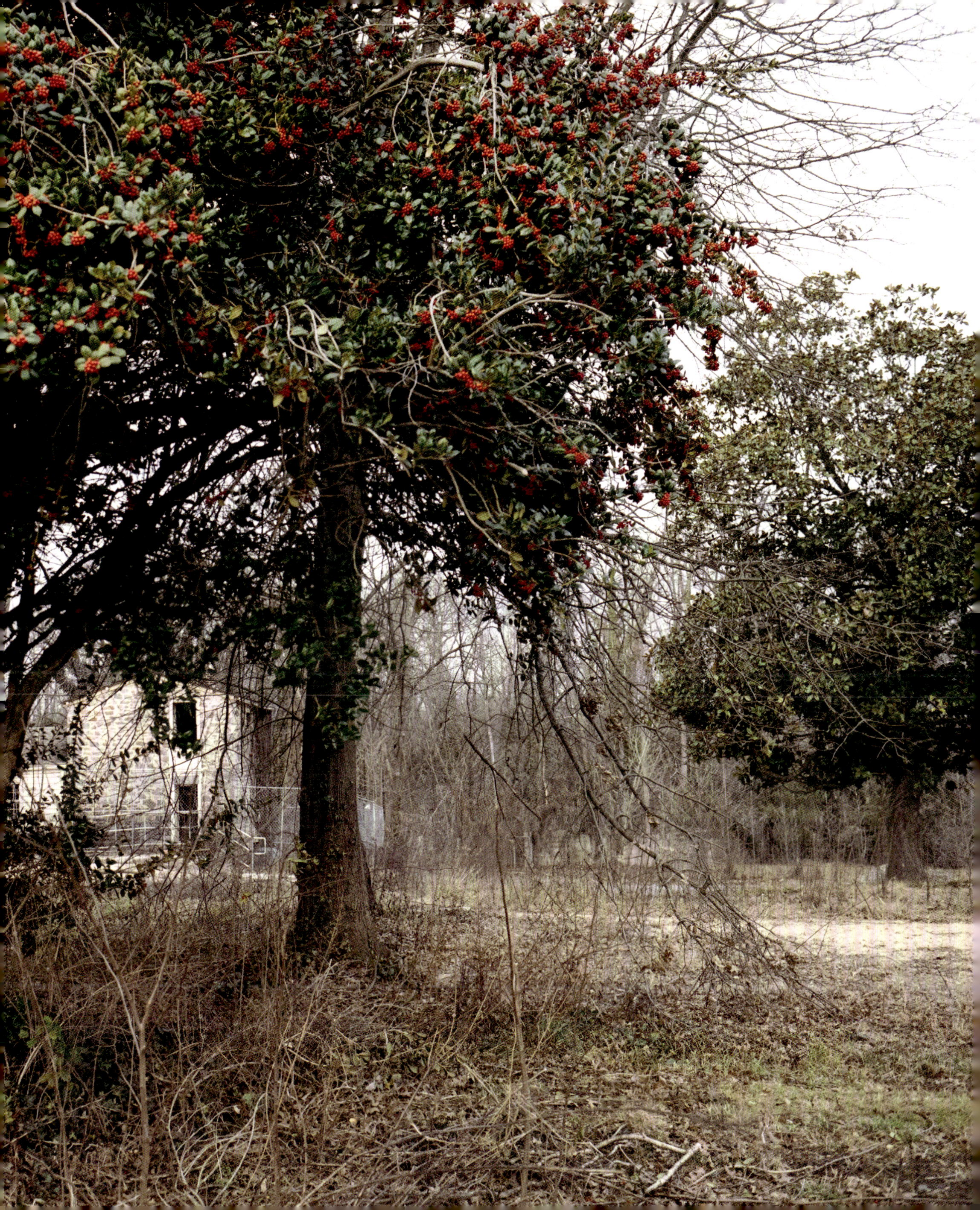

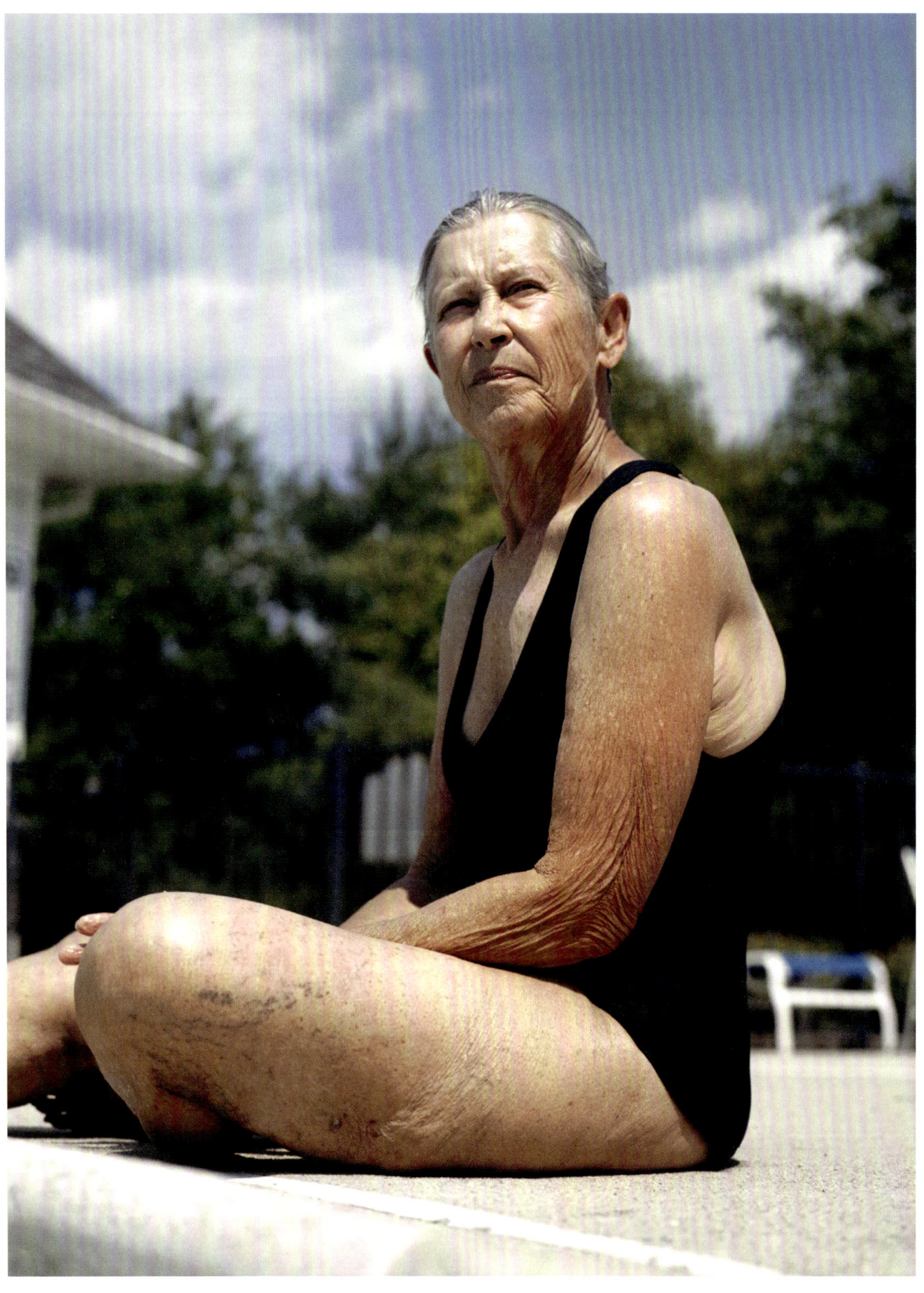

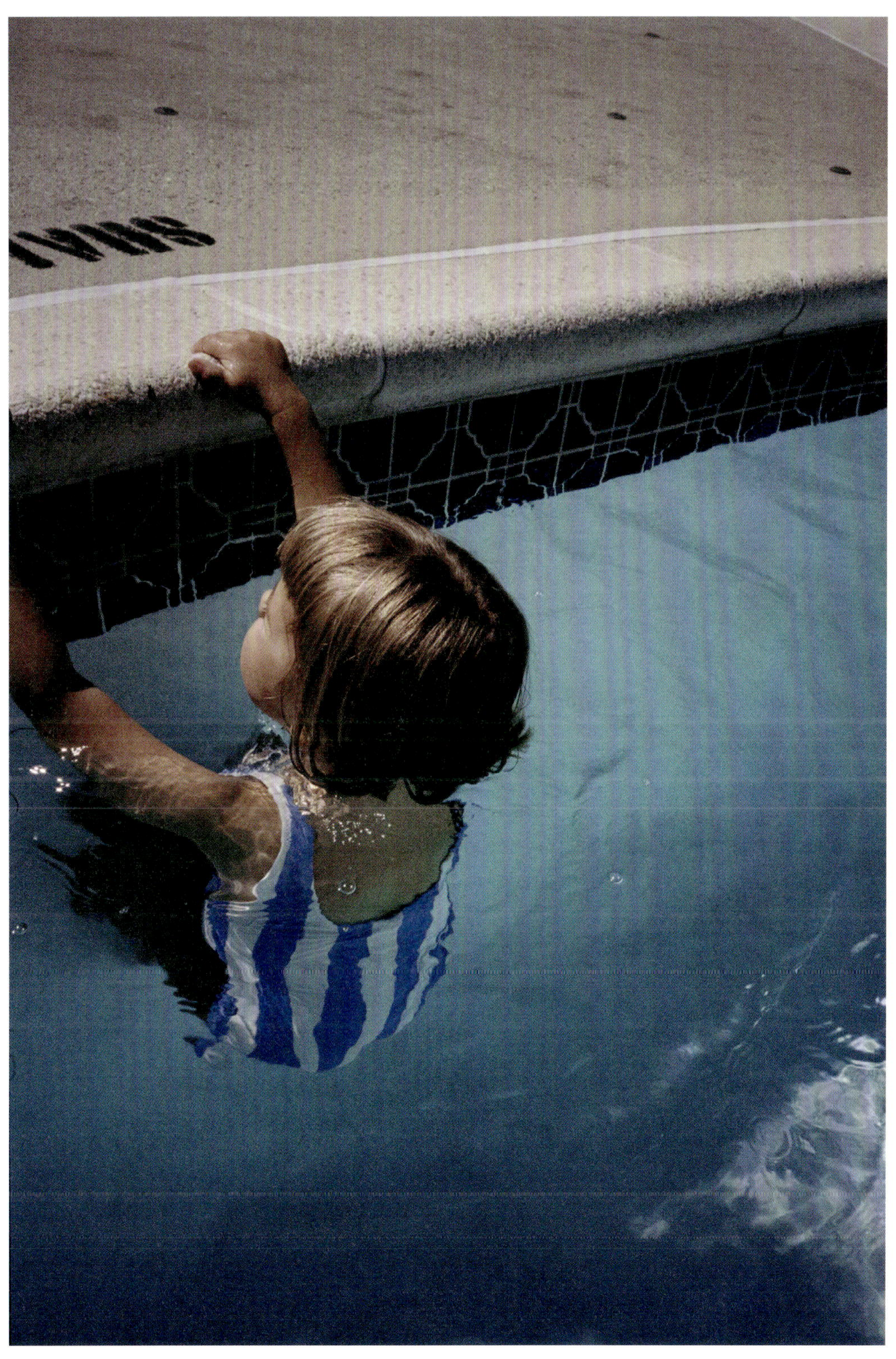

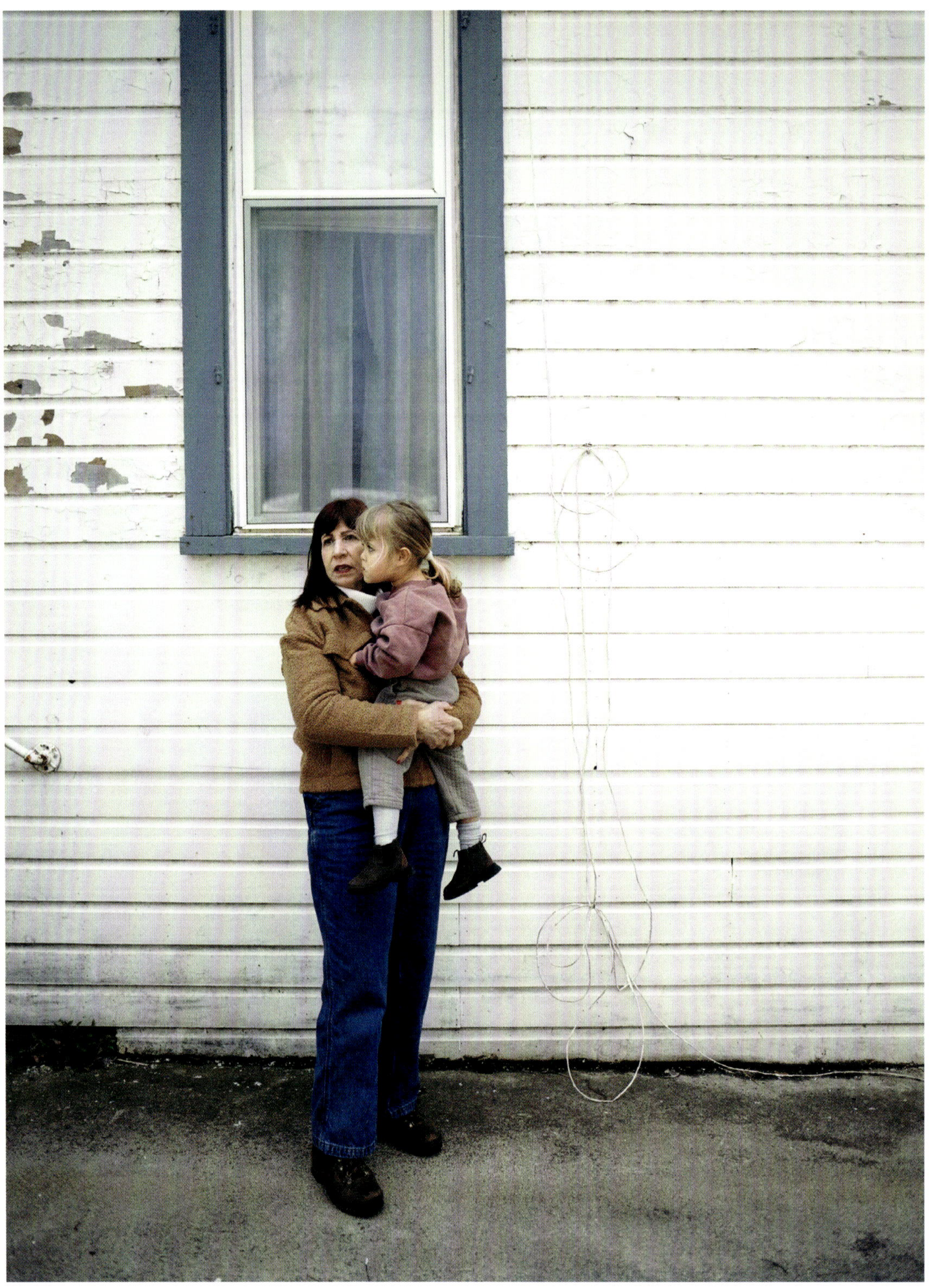

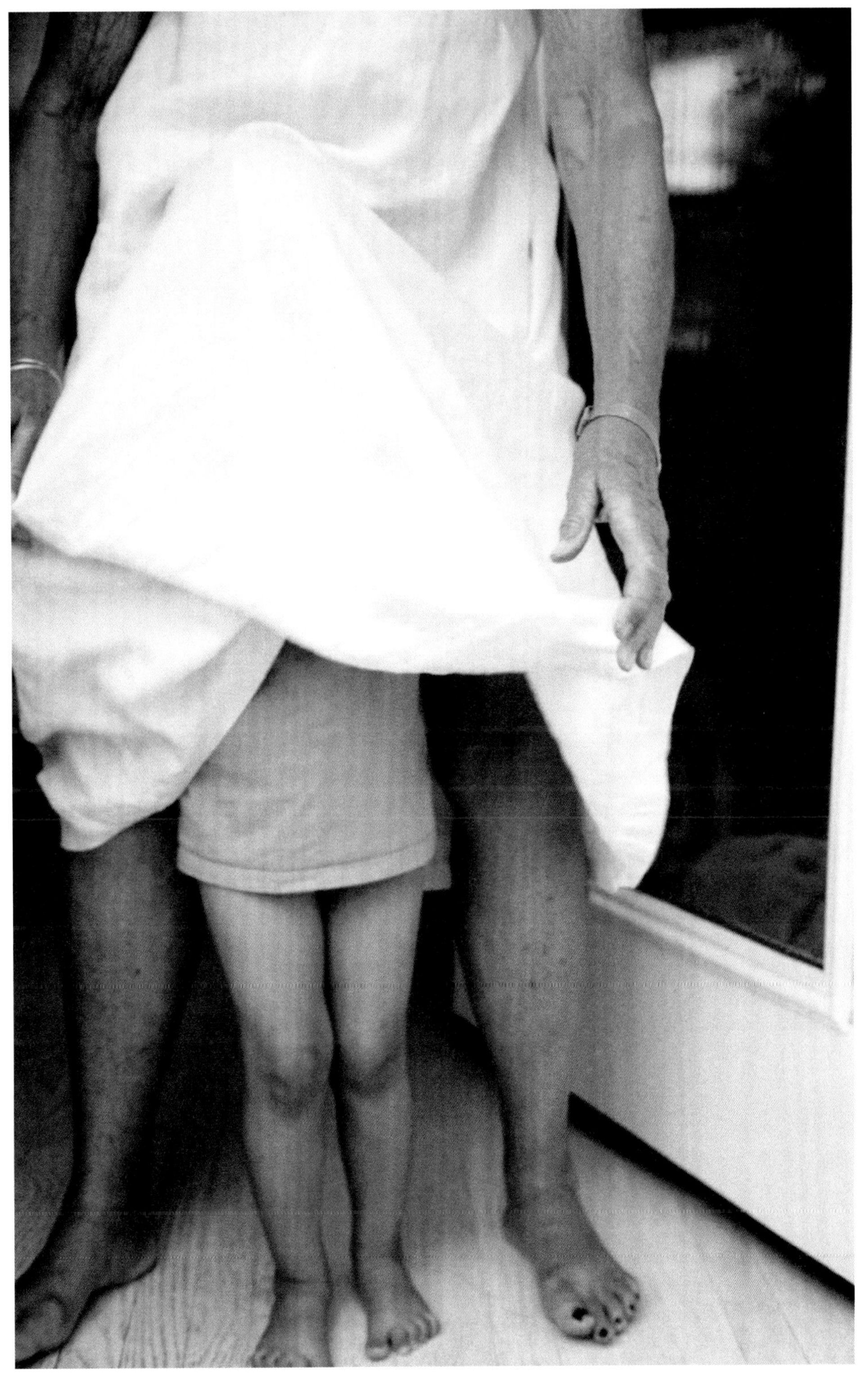

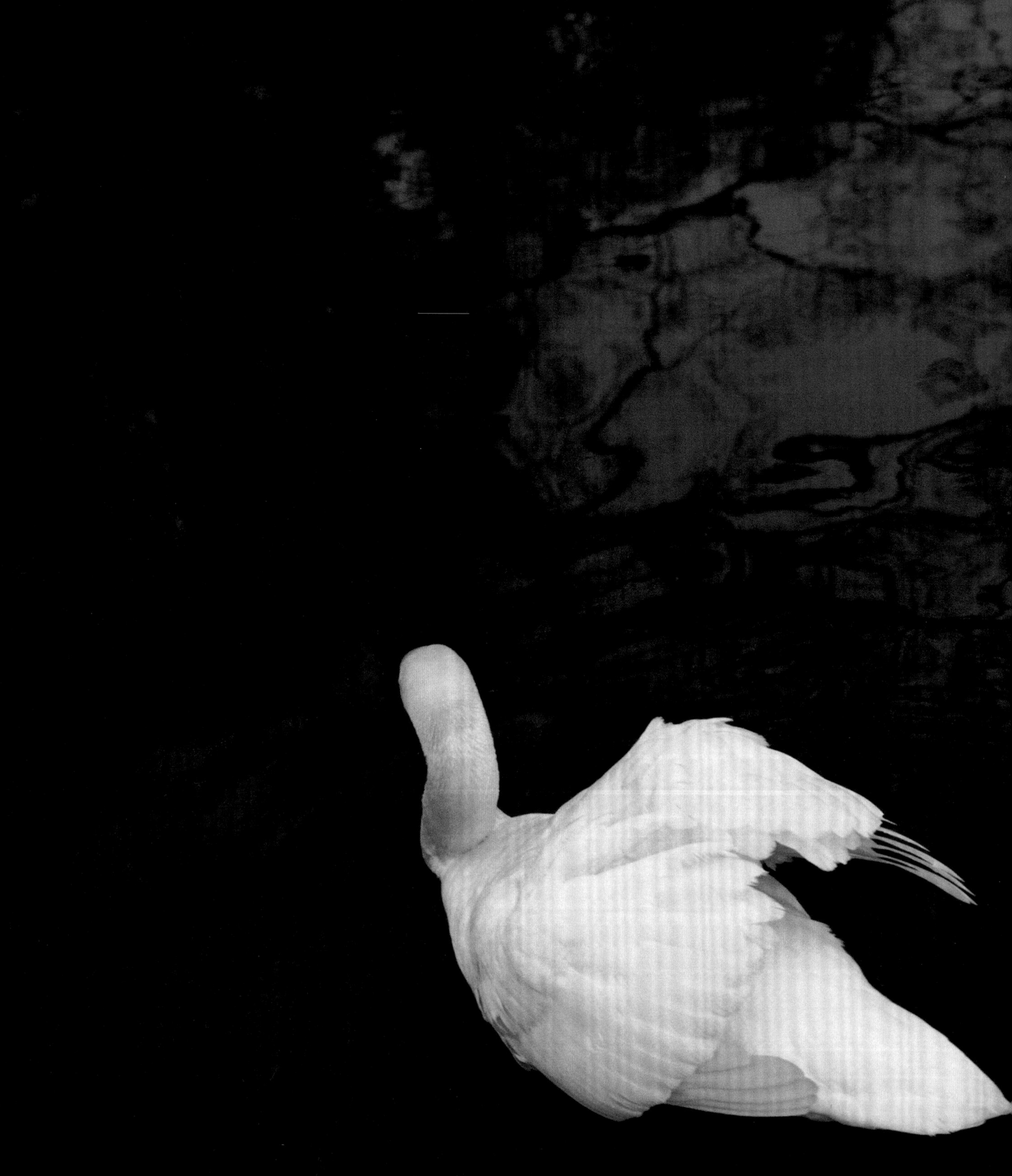

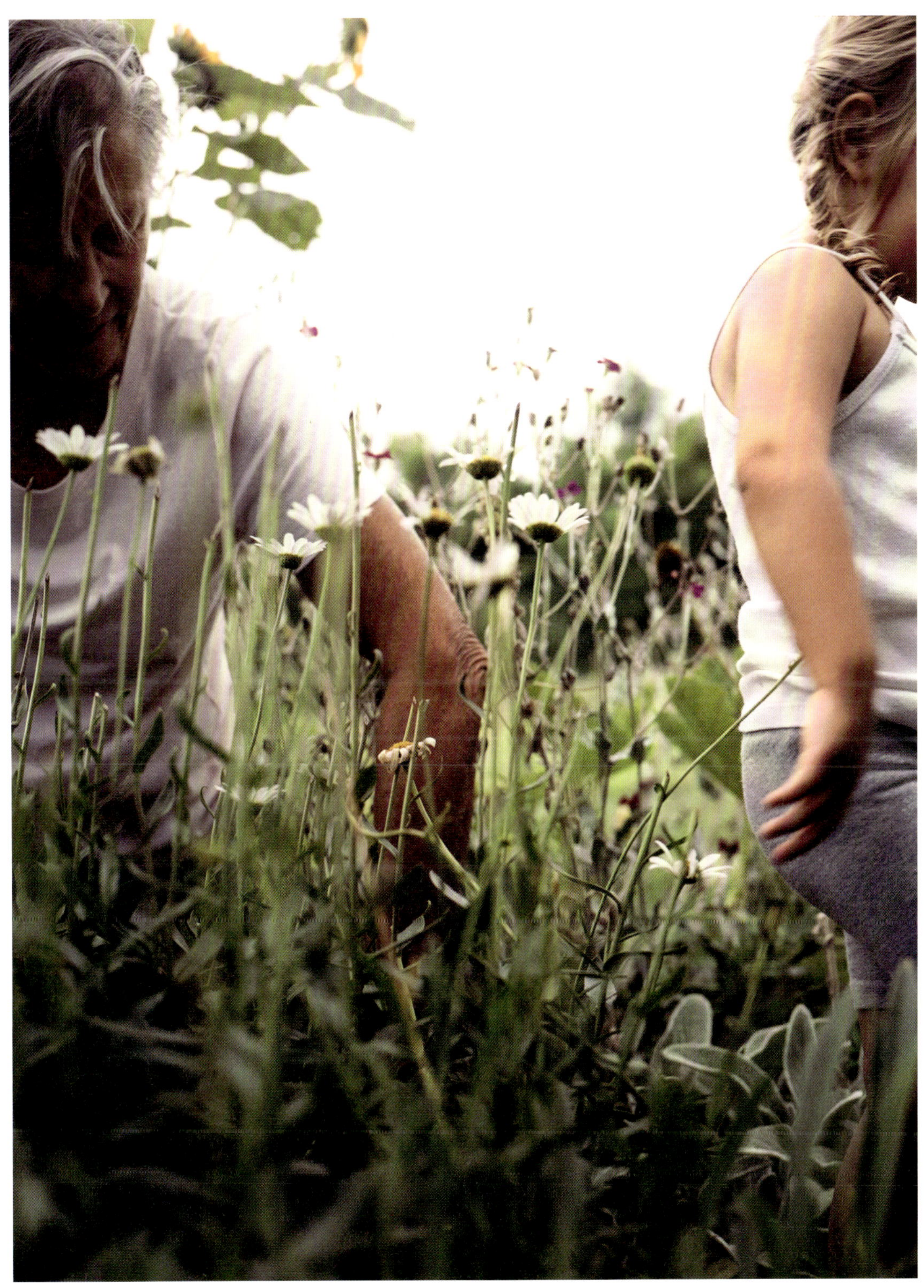

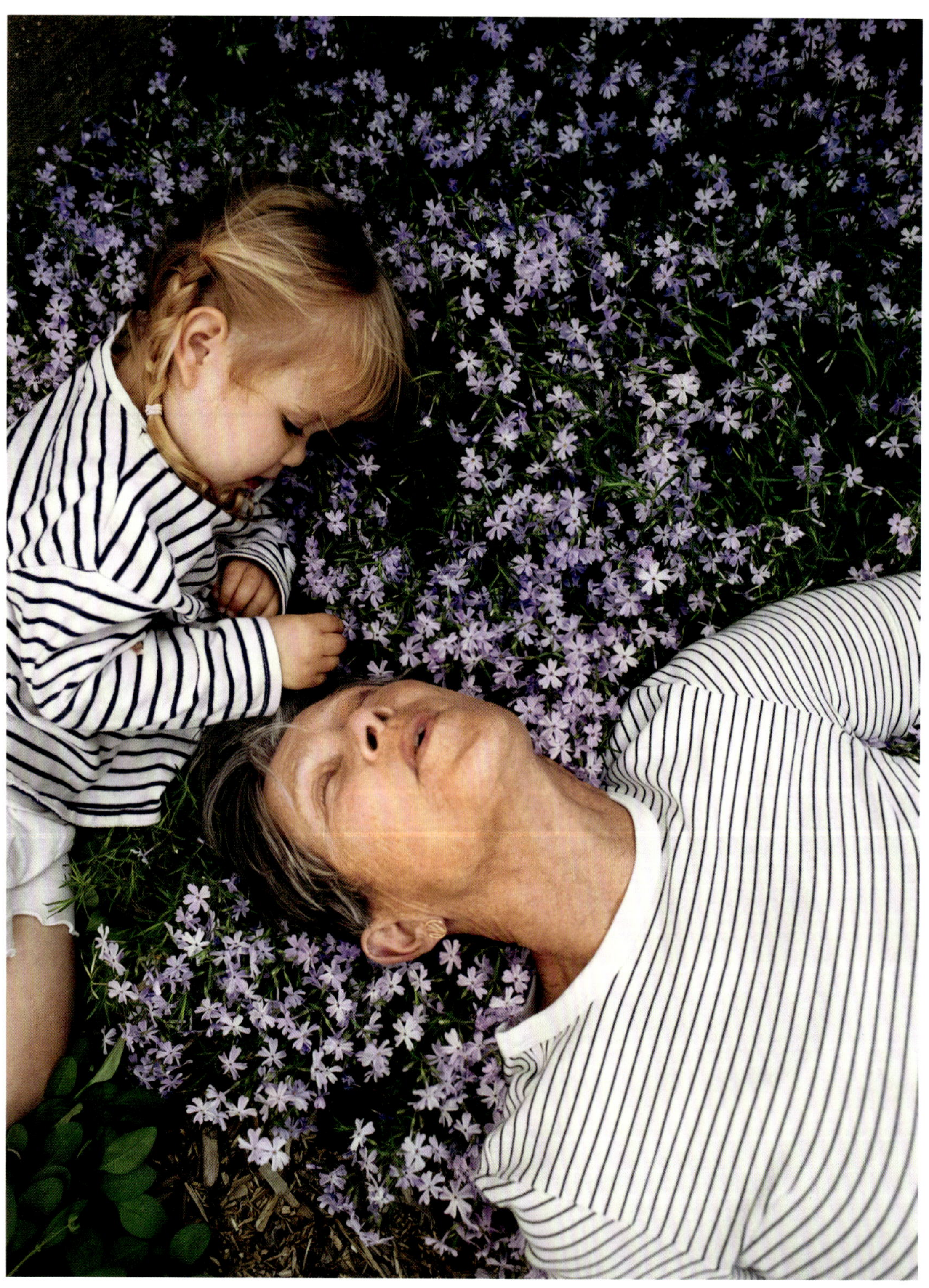

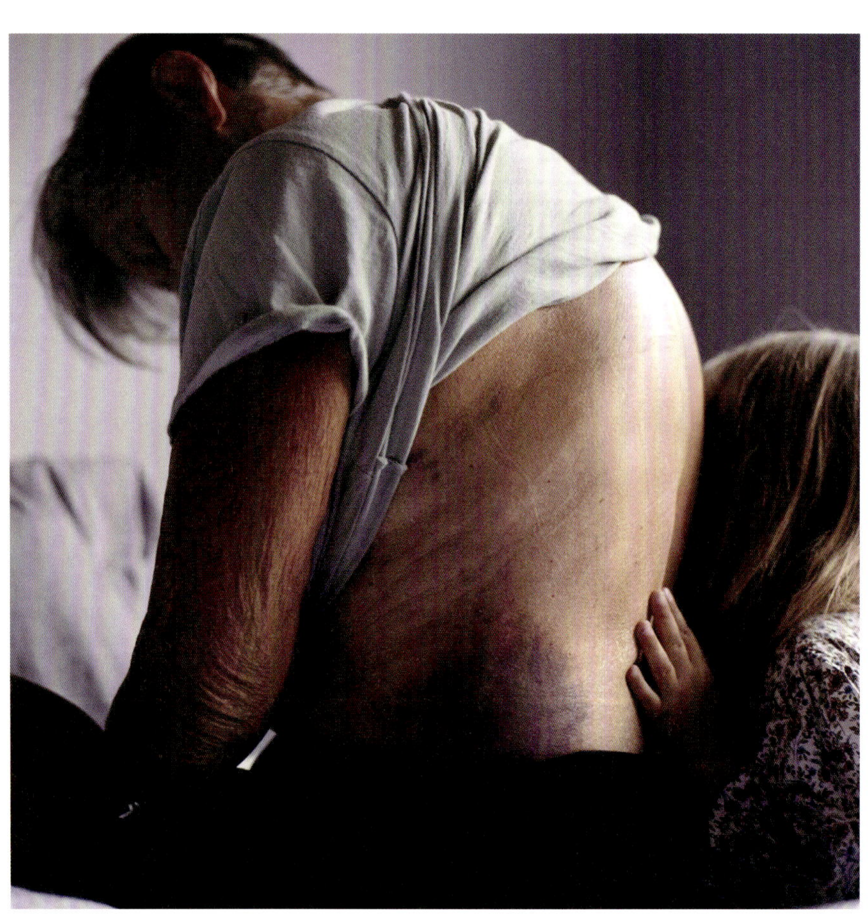

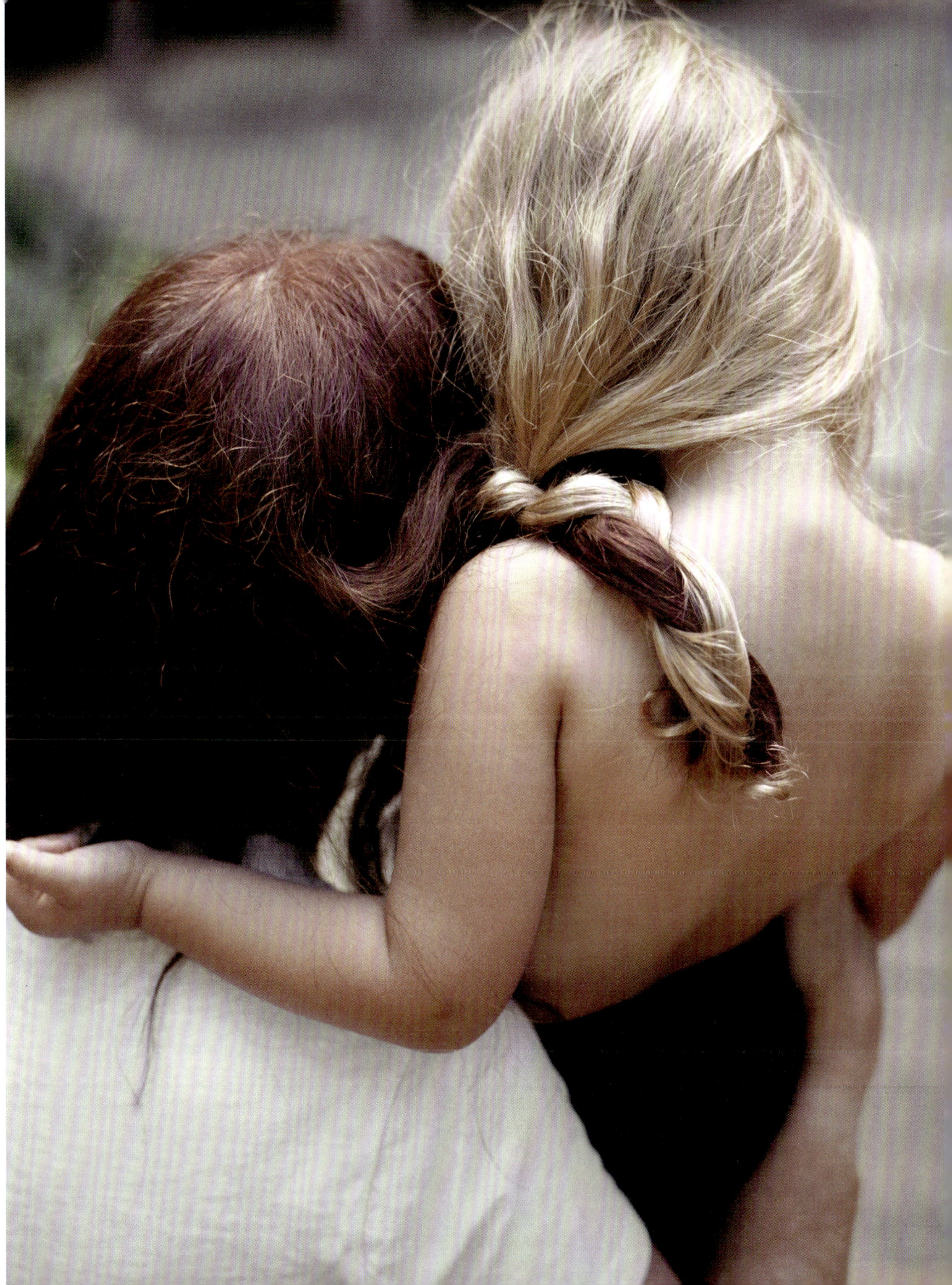

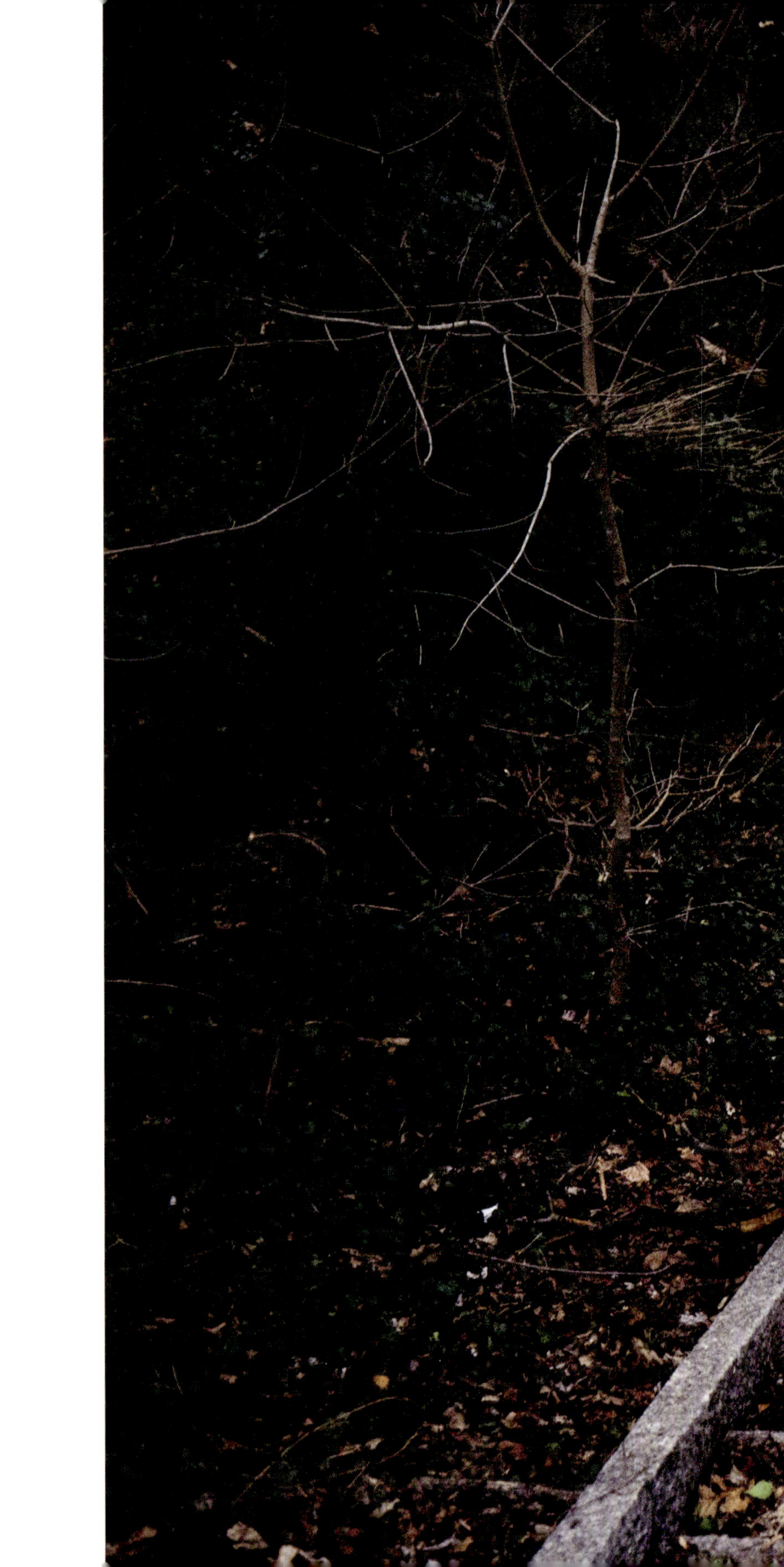

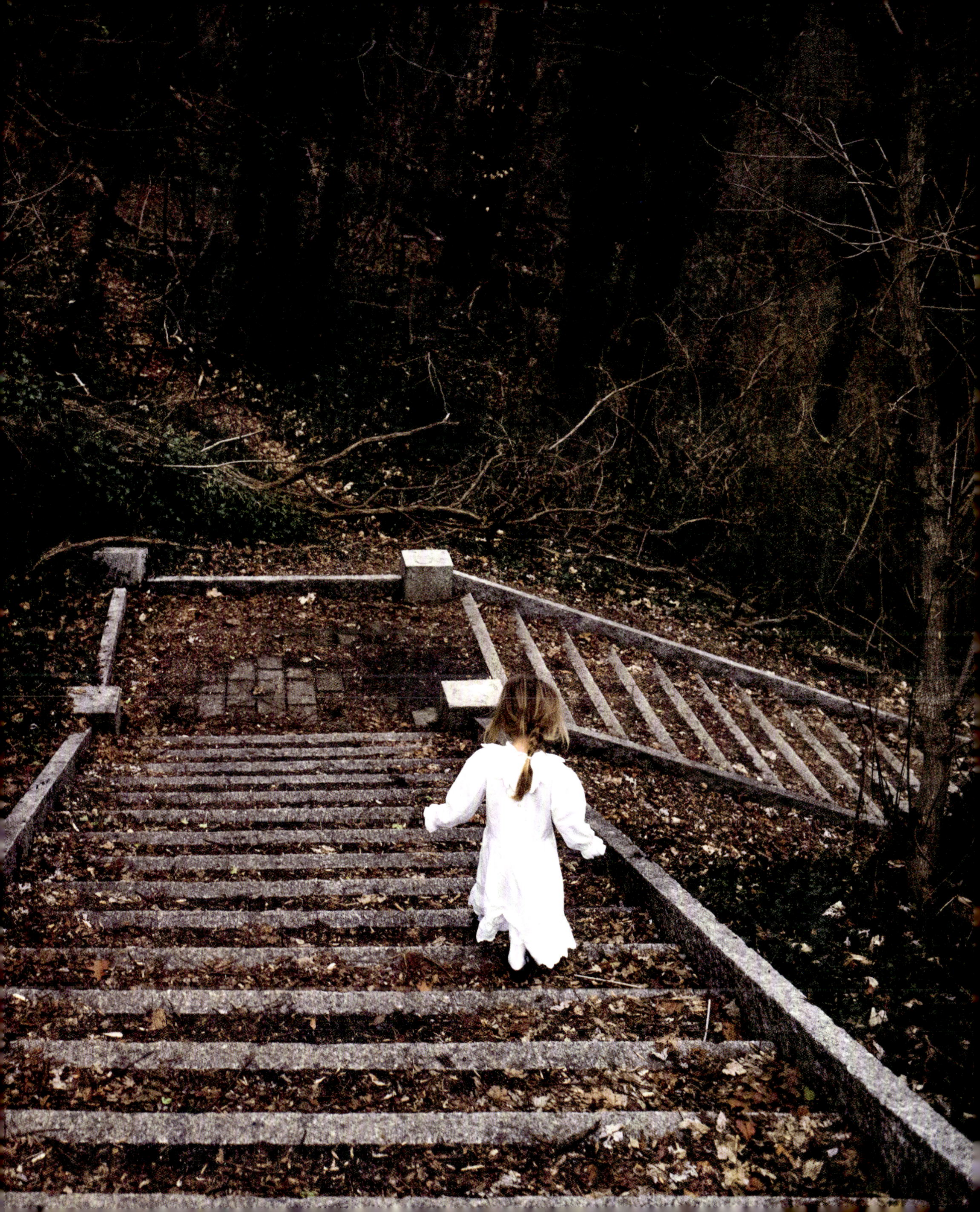

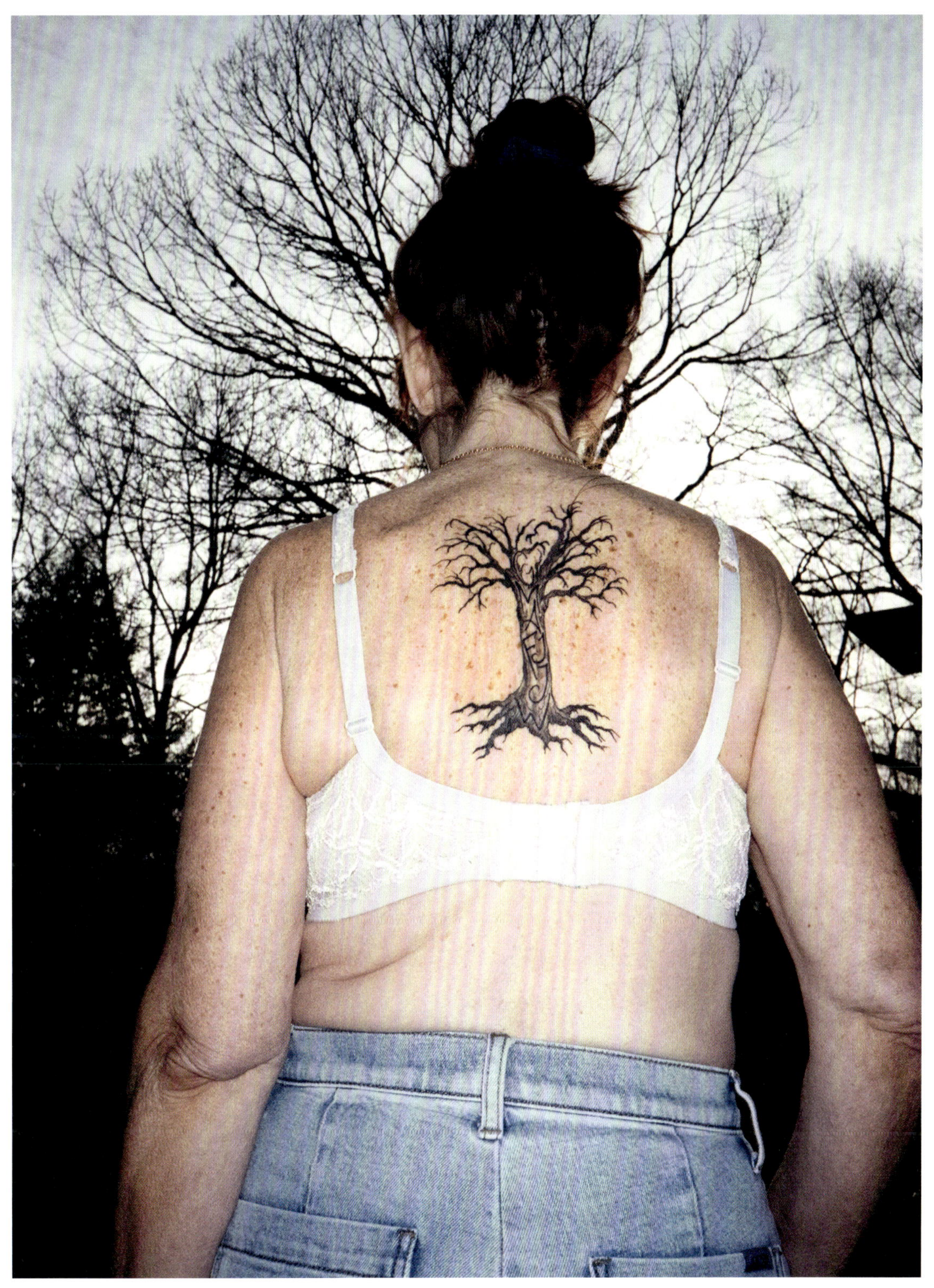

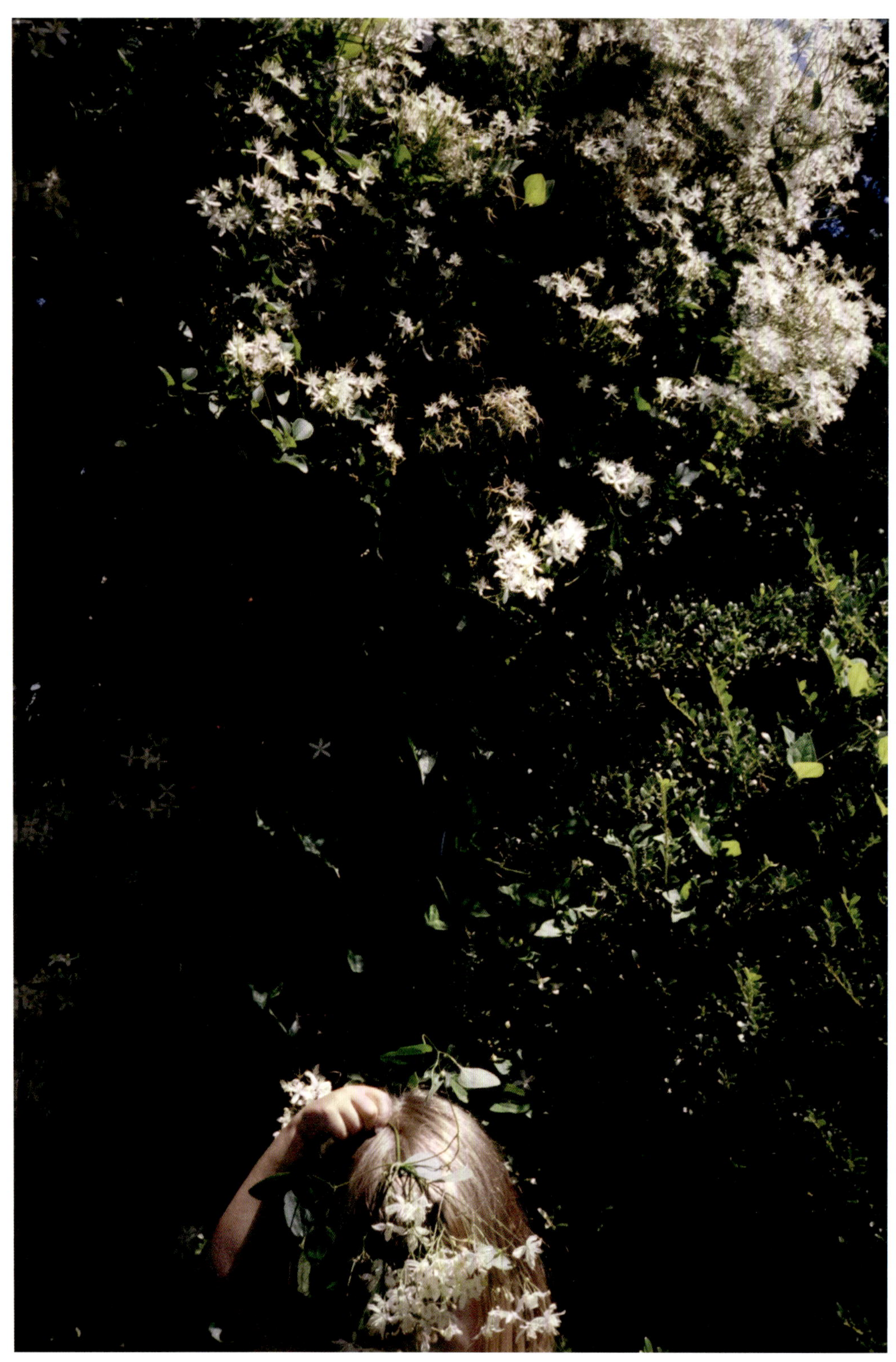

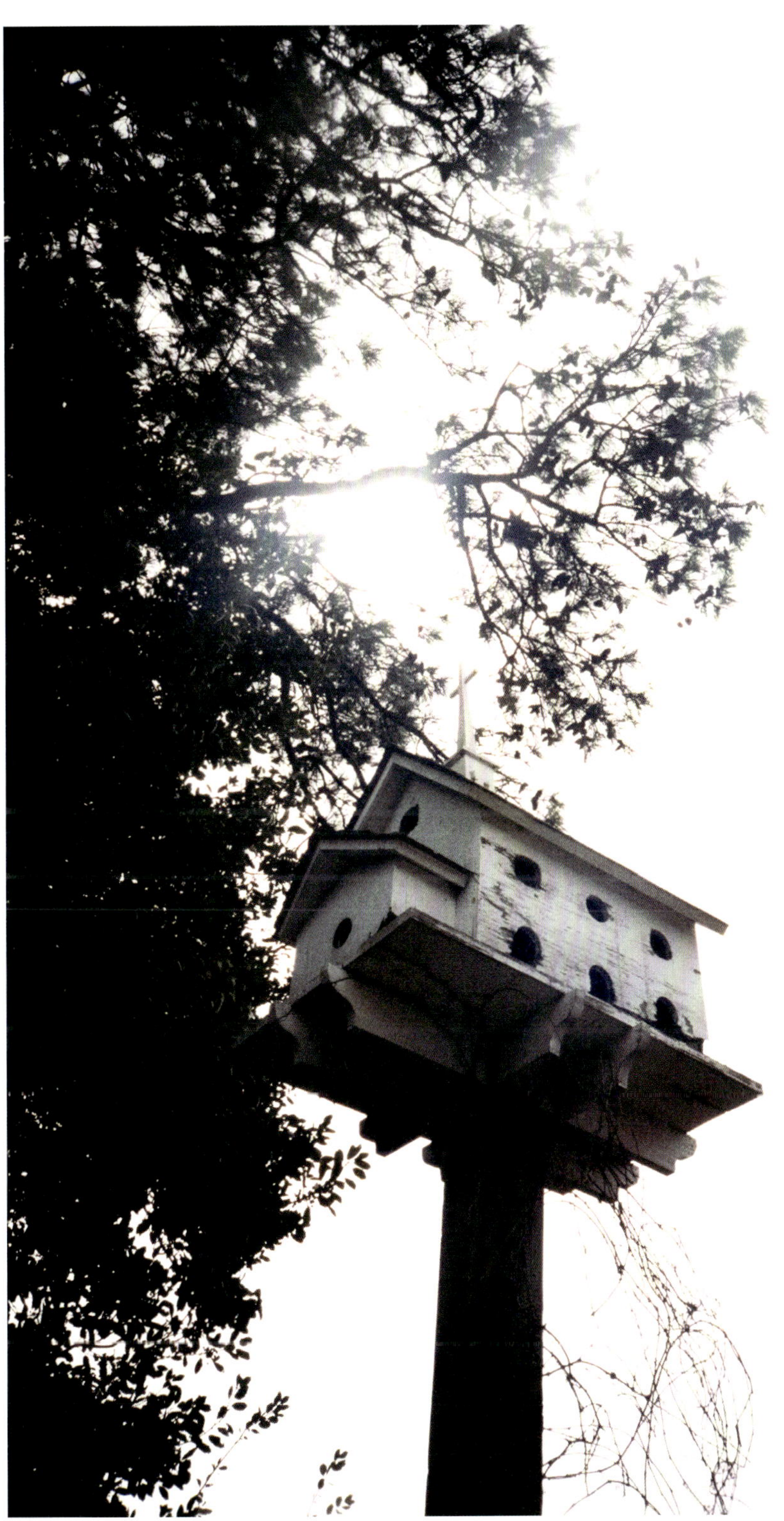

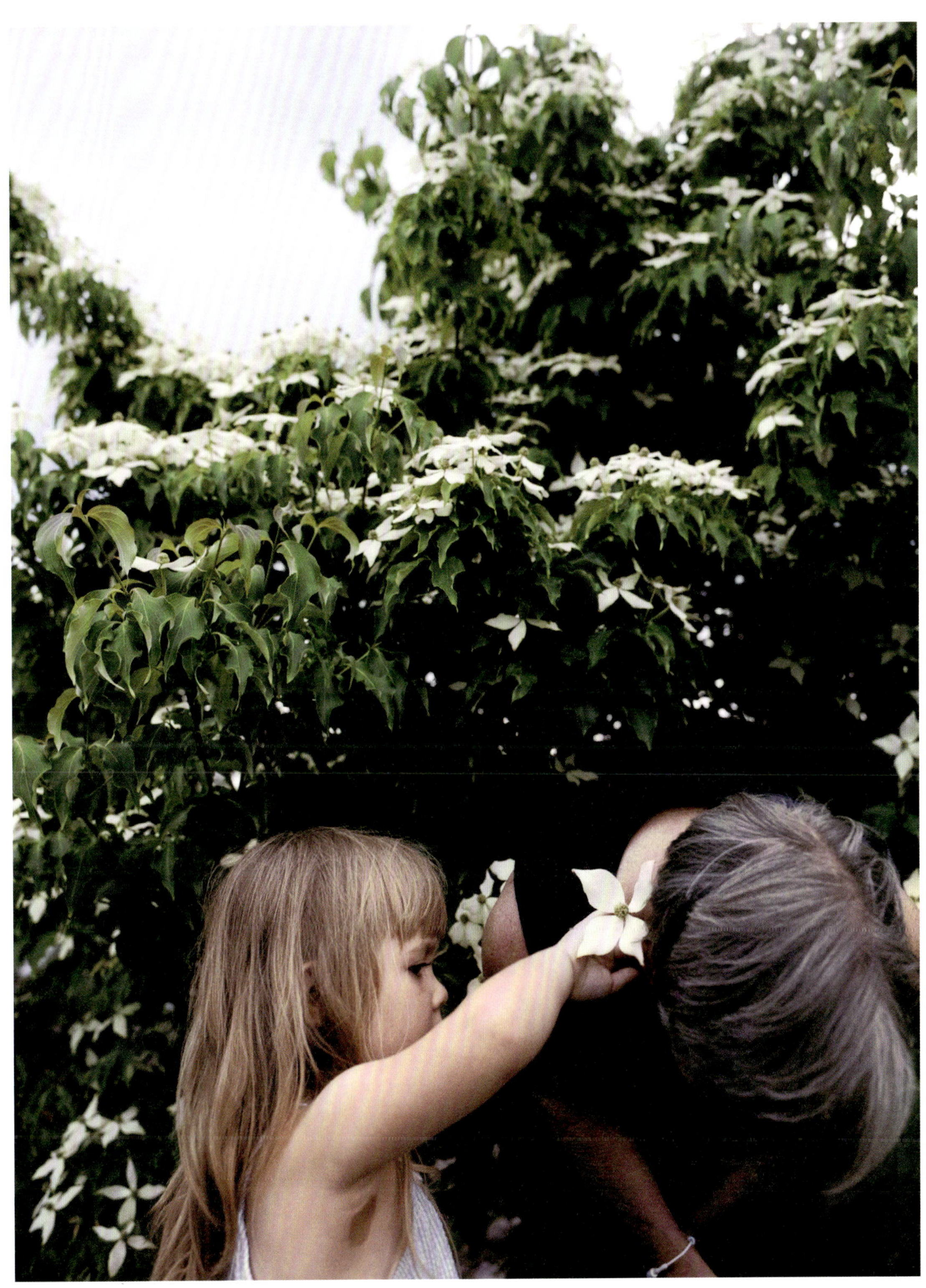

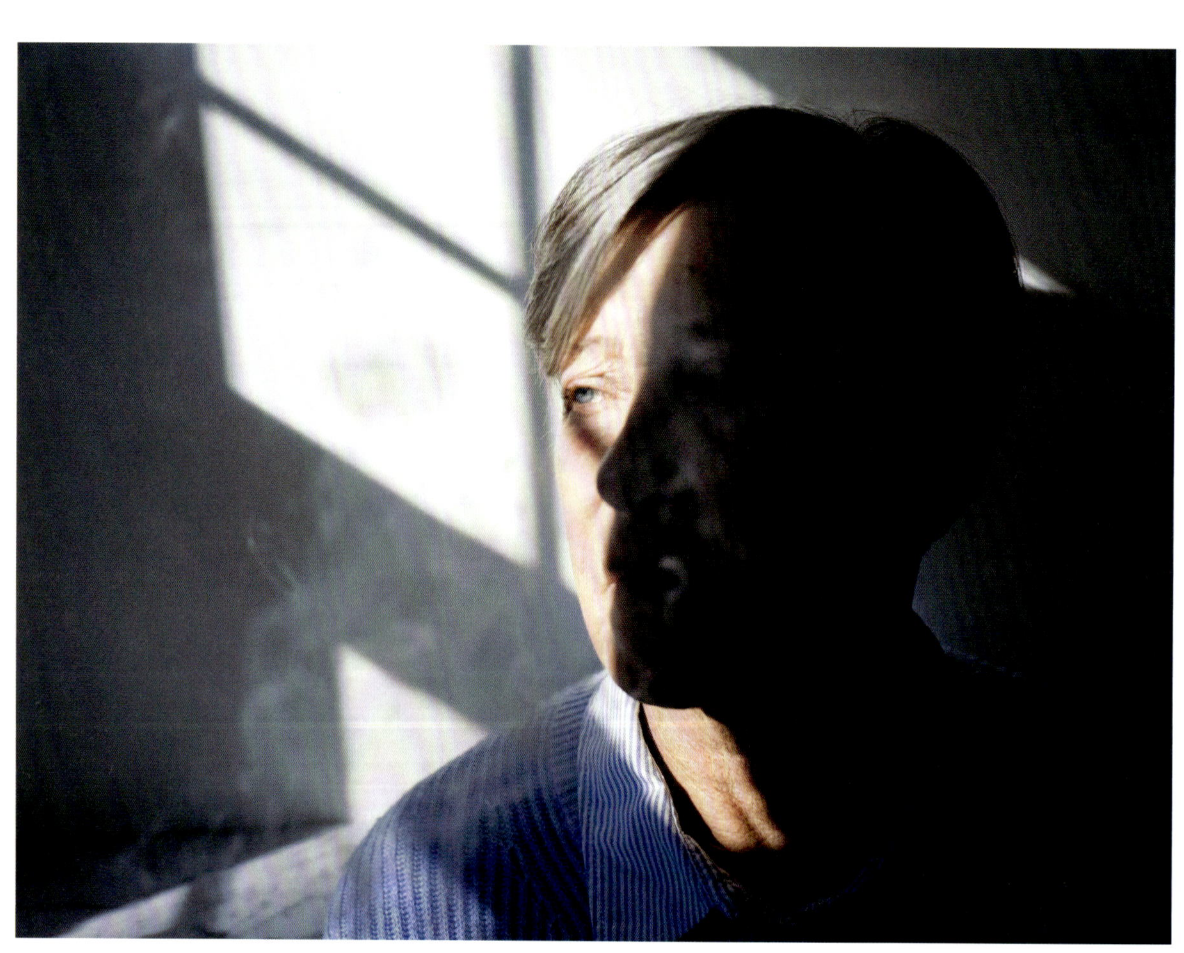

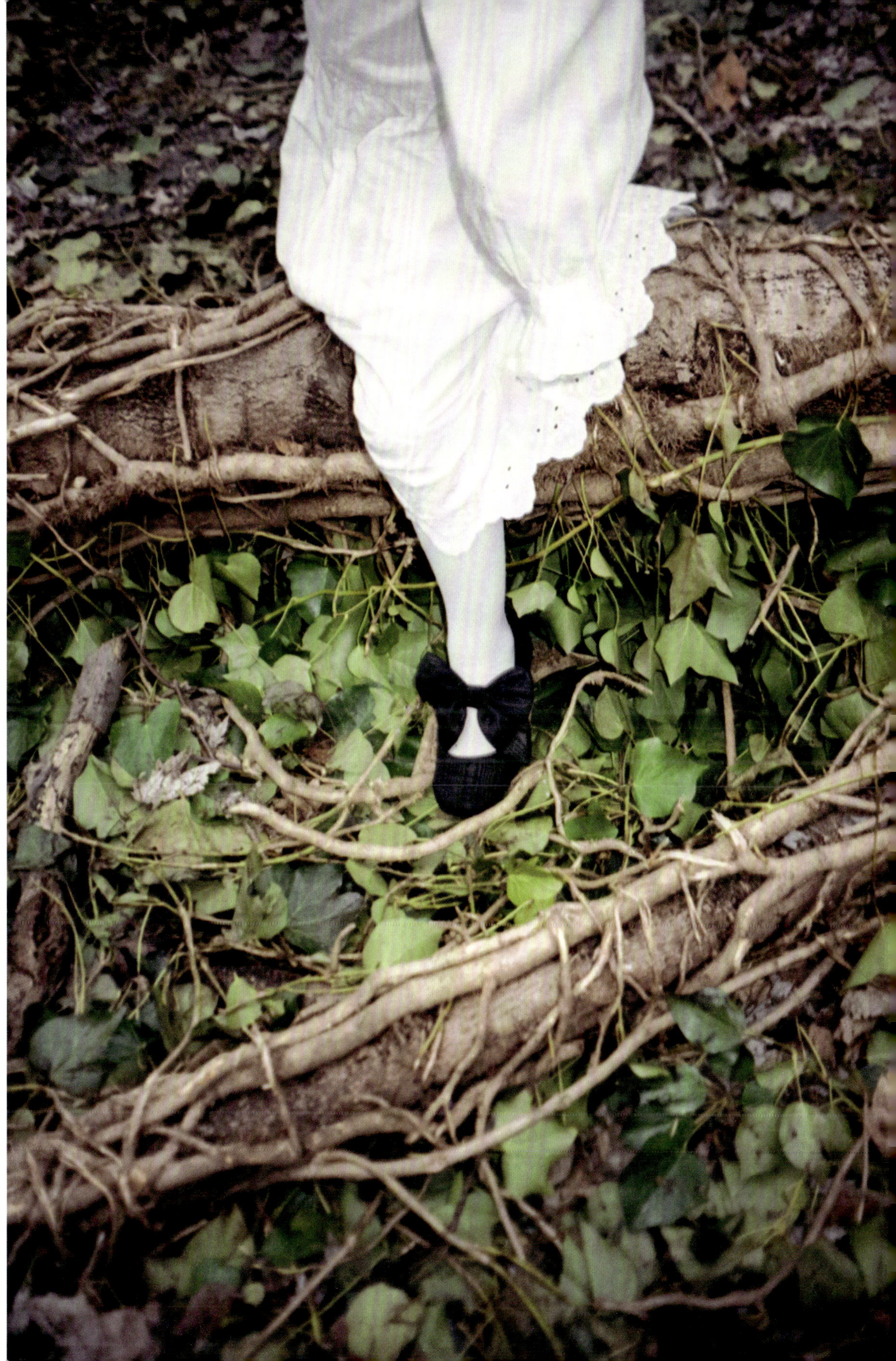

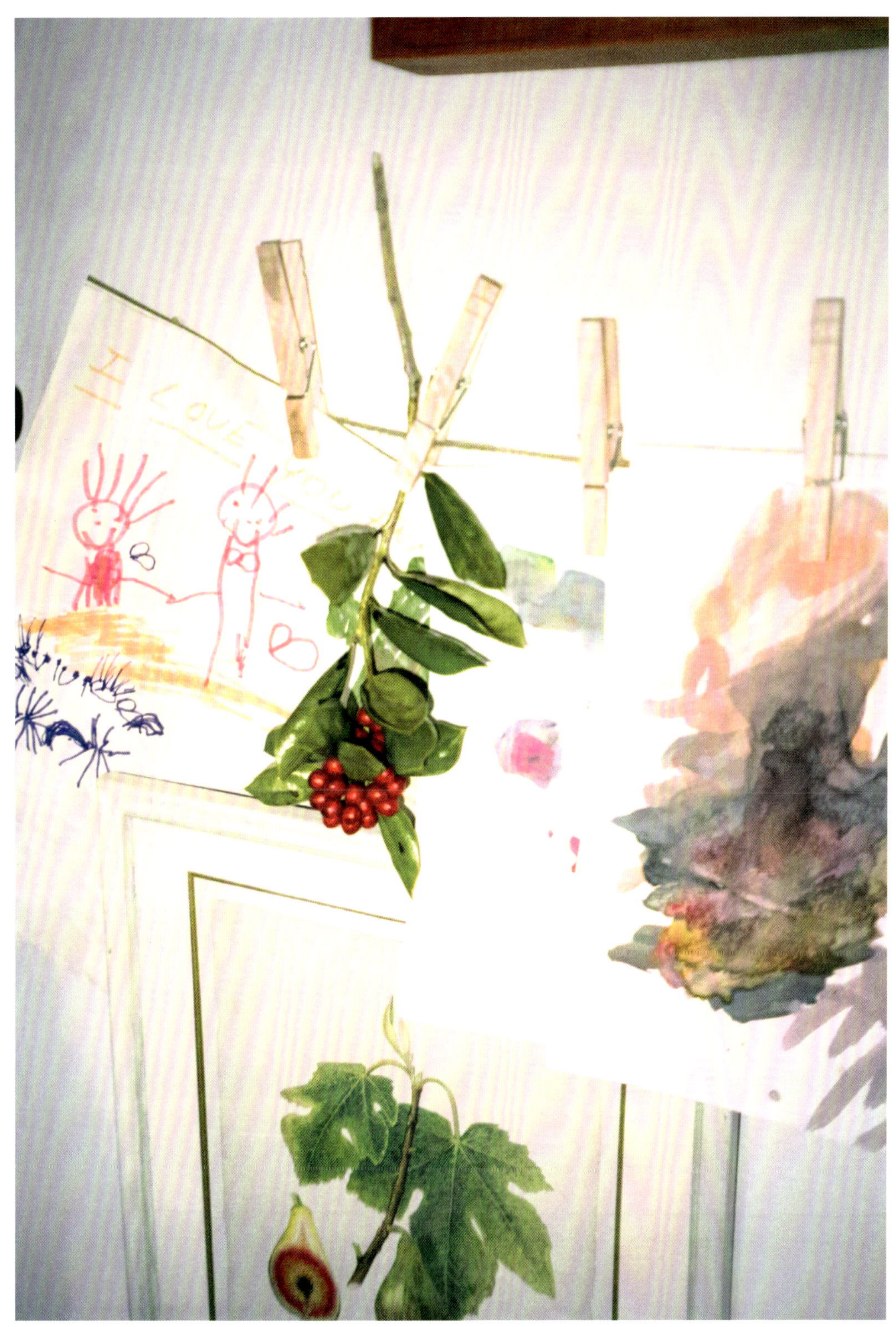
I LOVE YOU

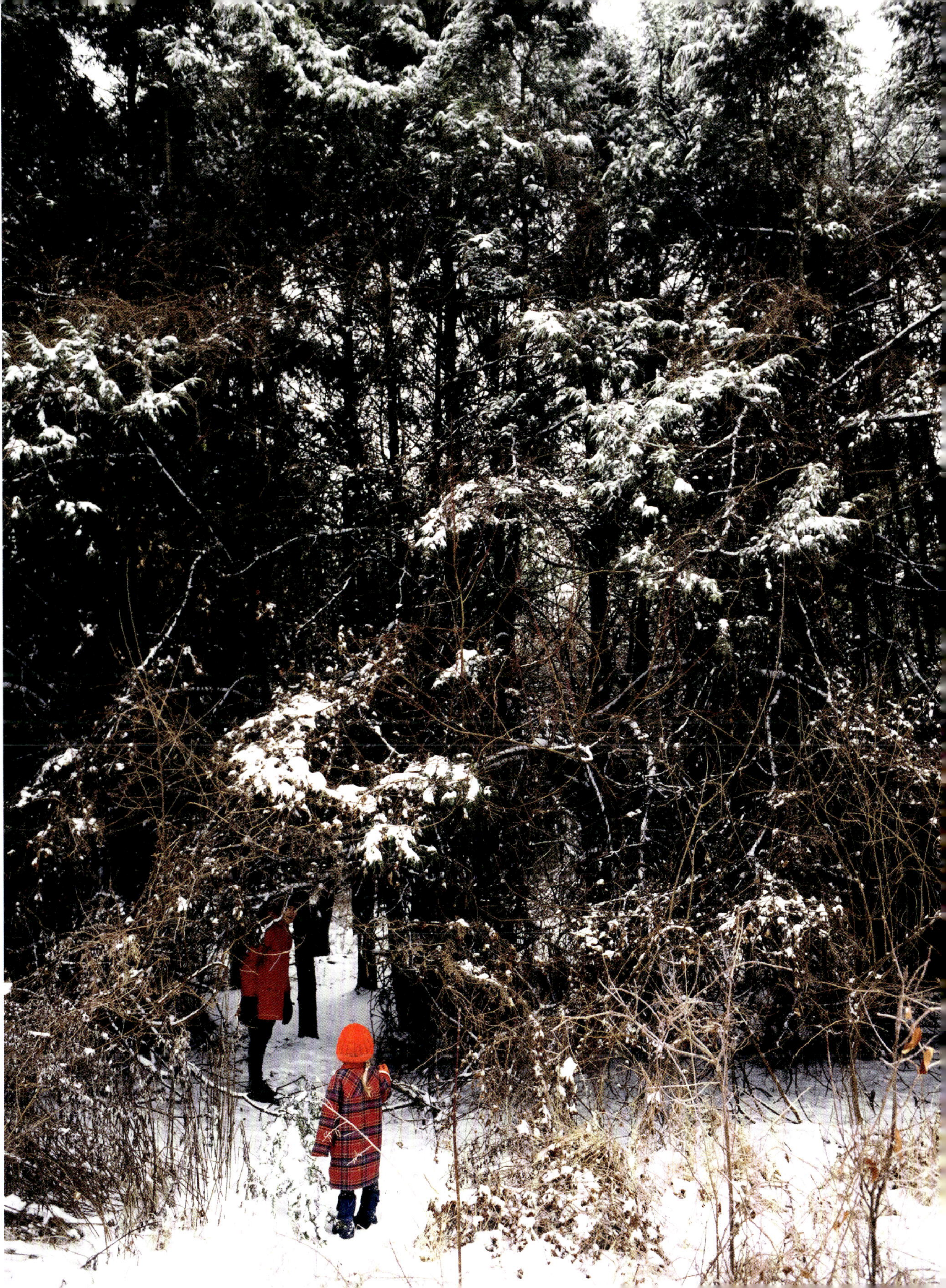

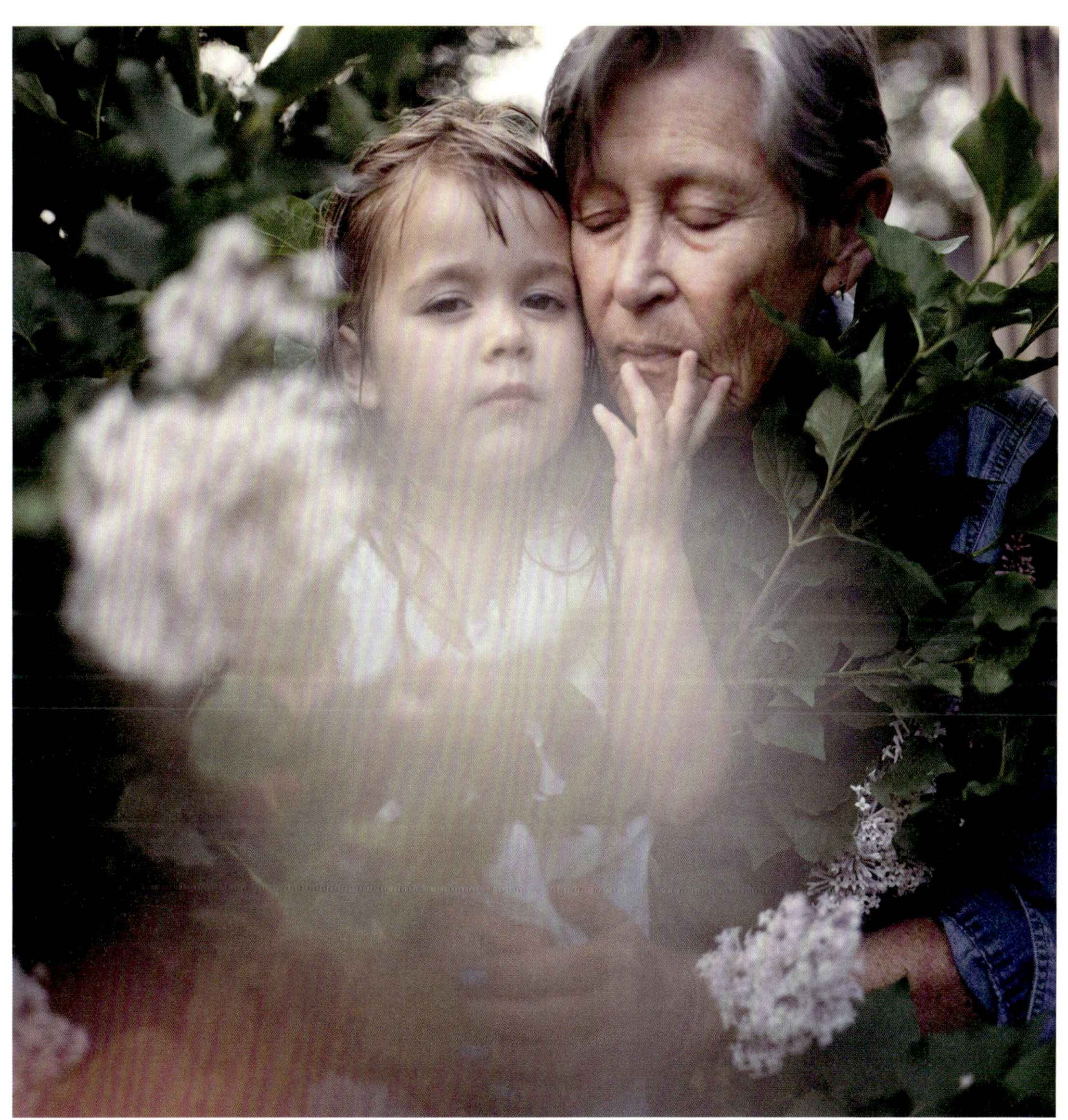

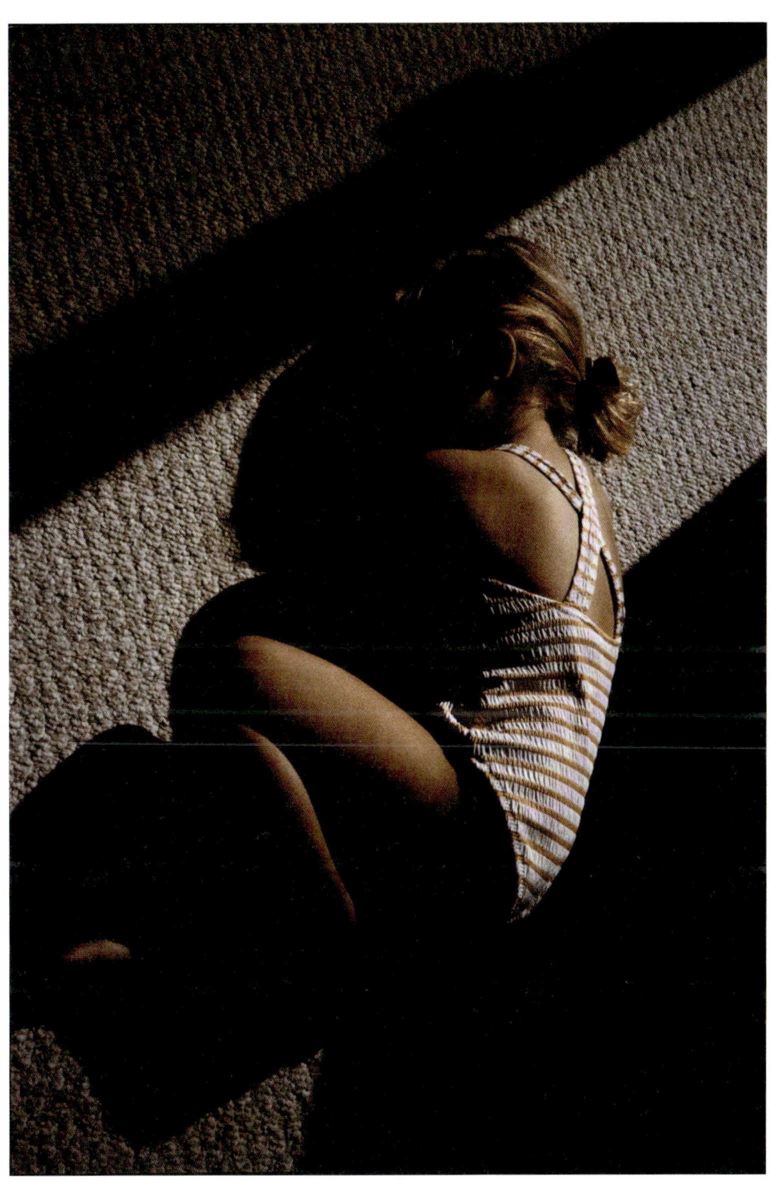

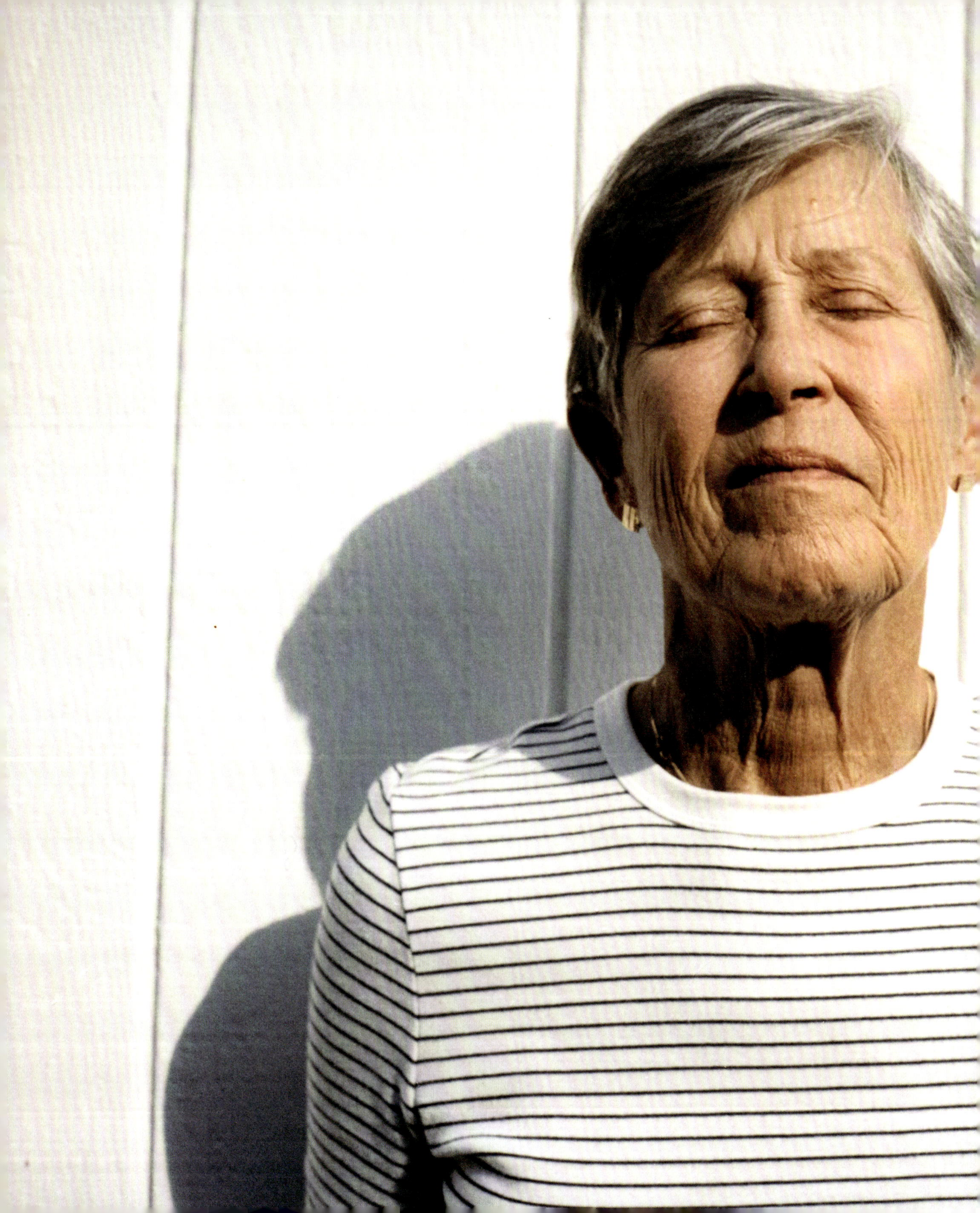

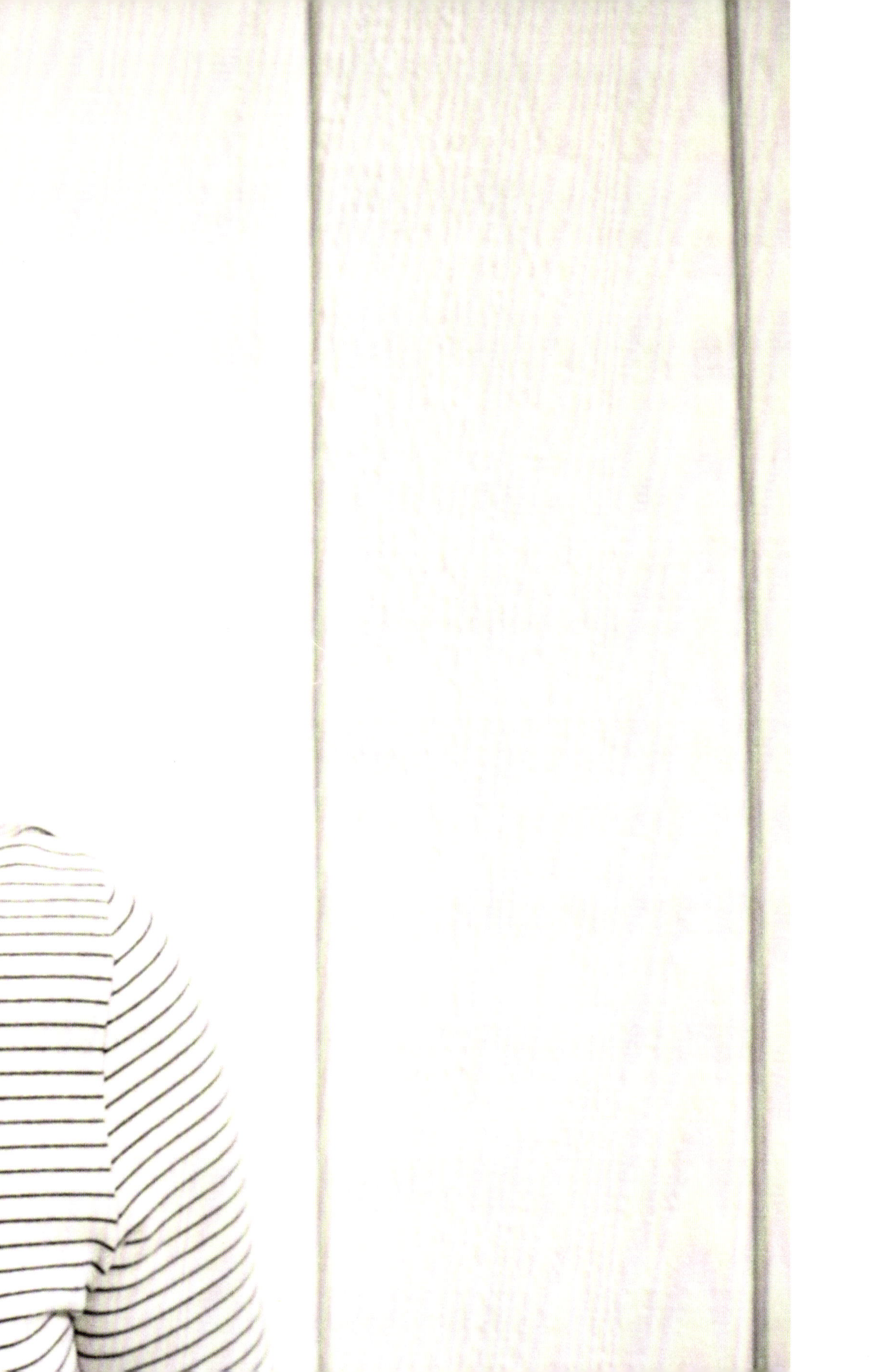

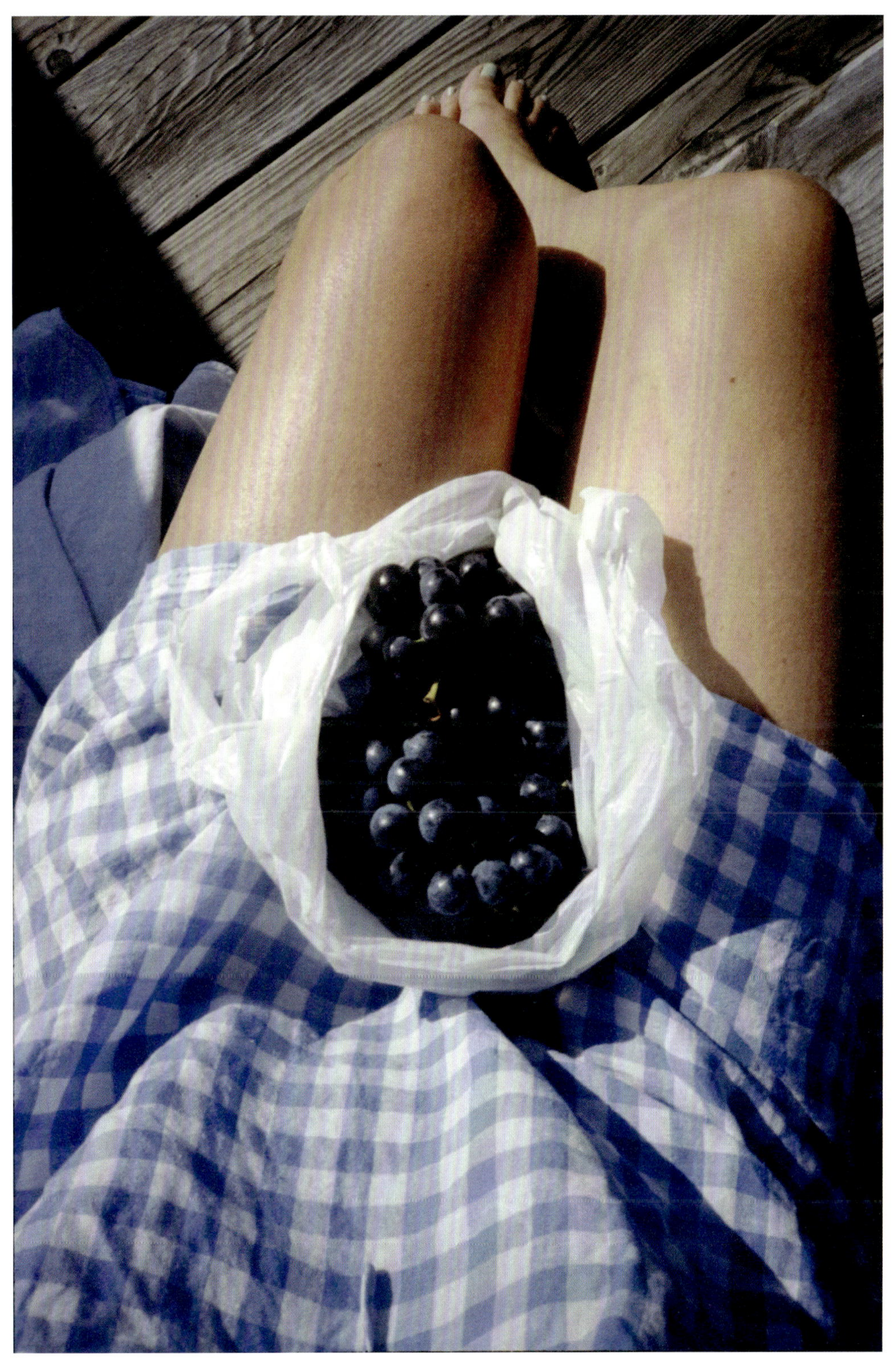

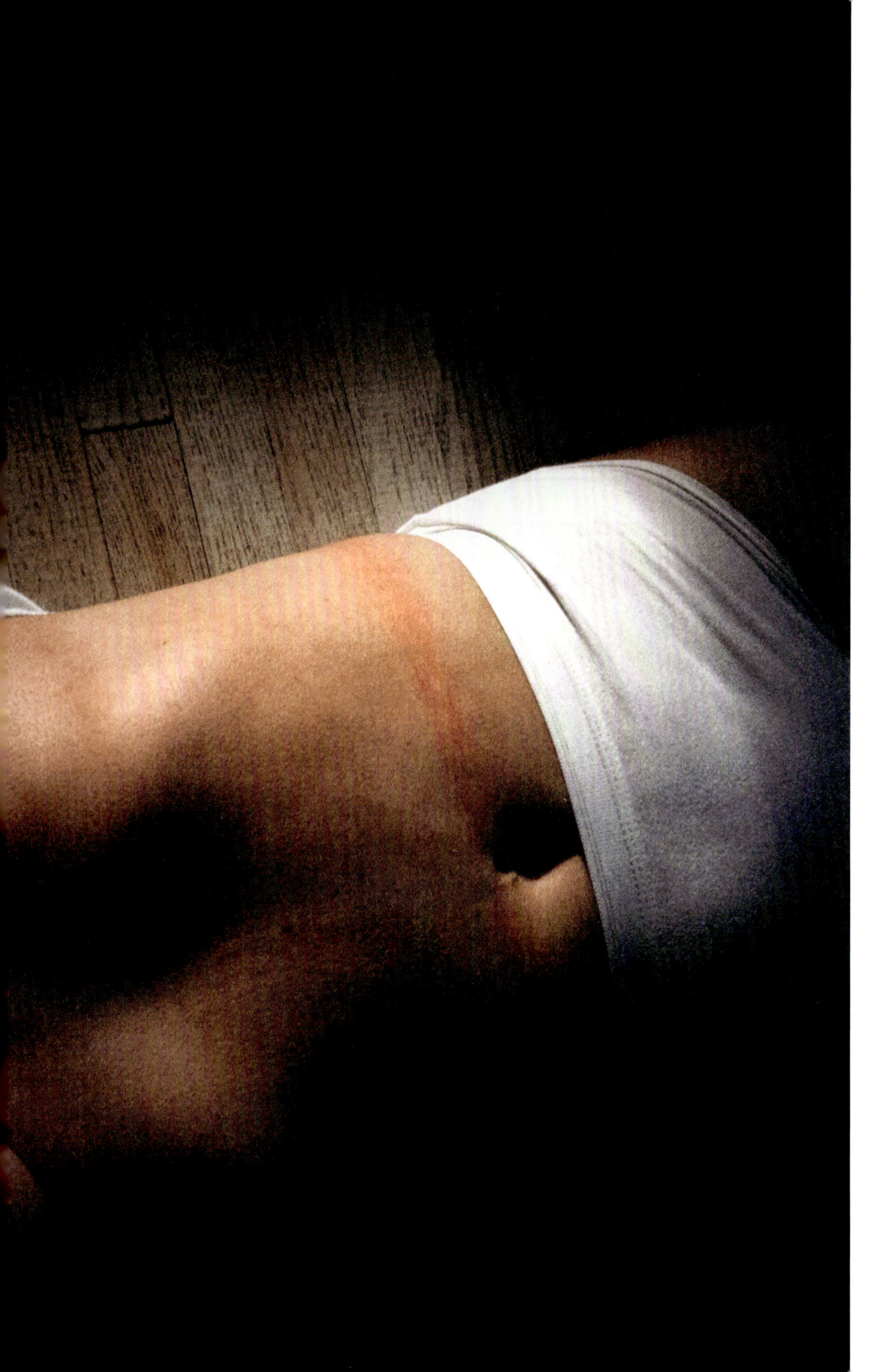

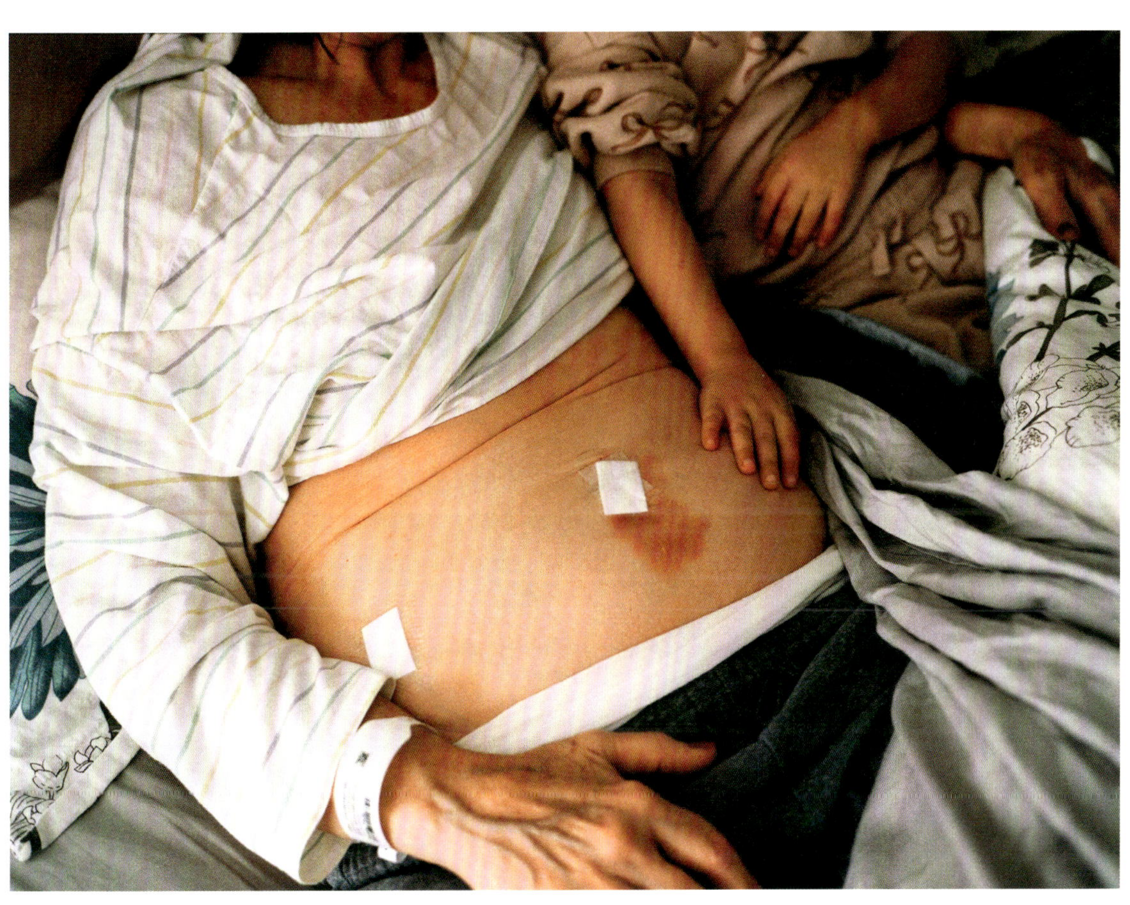

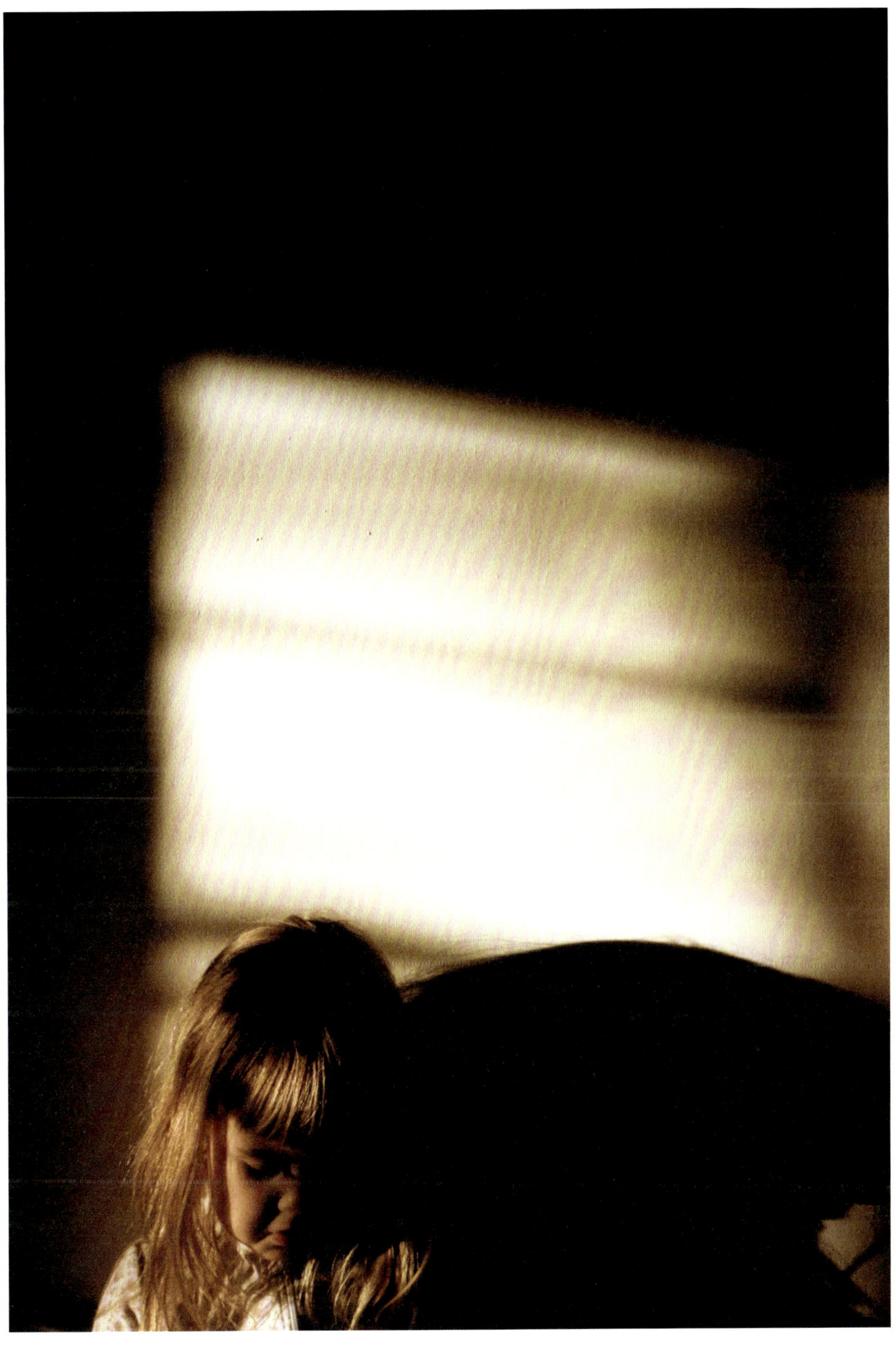

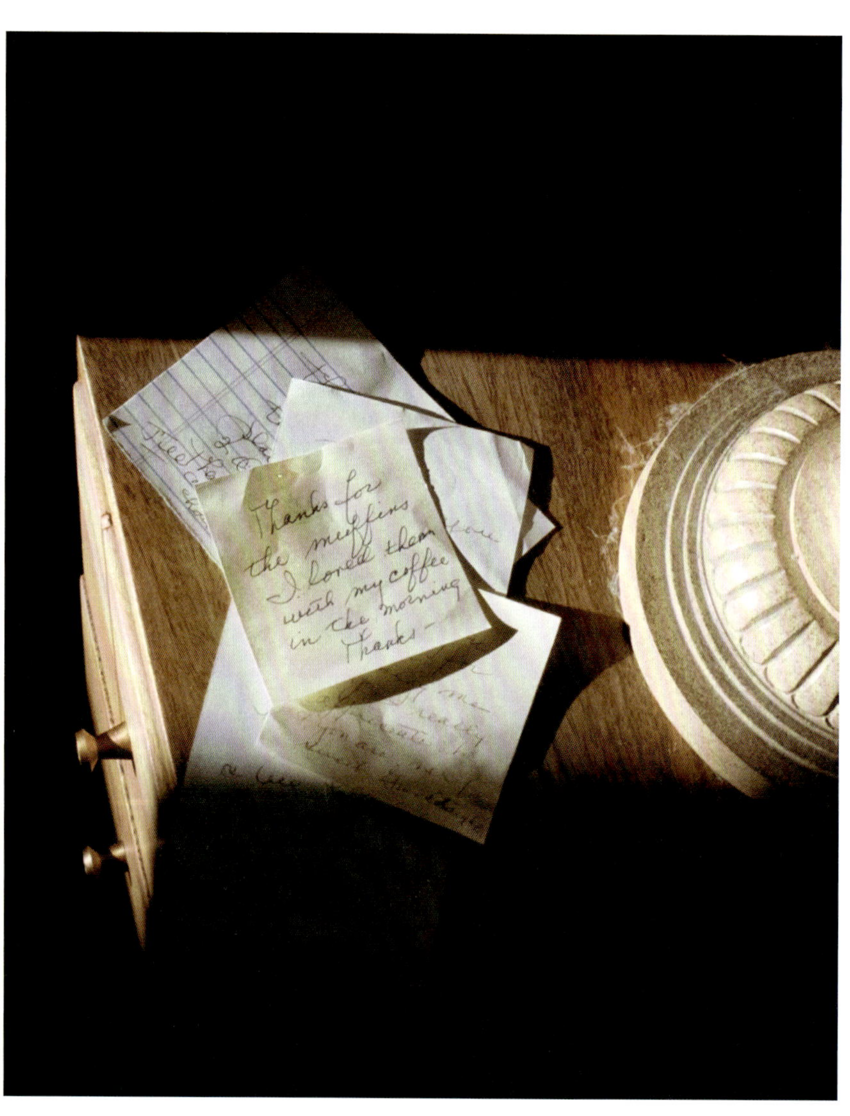
Thanks for
the muffins
I loved them
with my coffee
in the morning
Thanks -

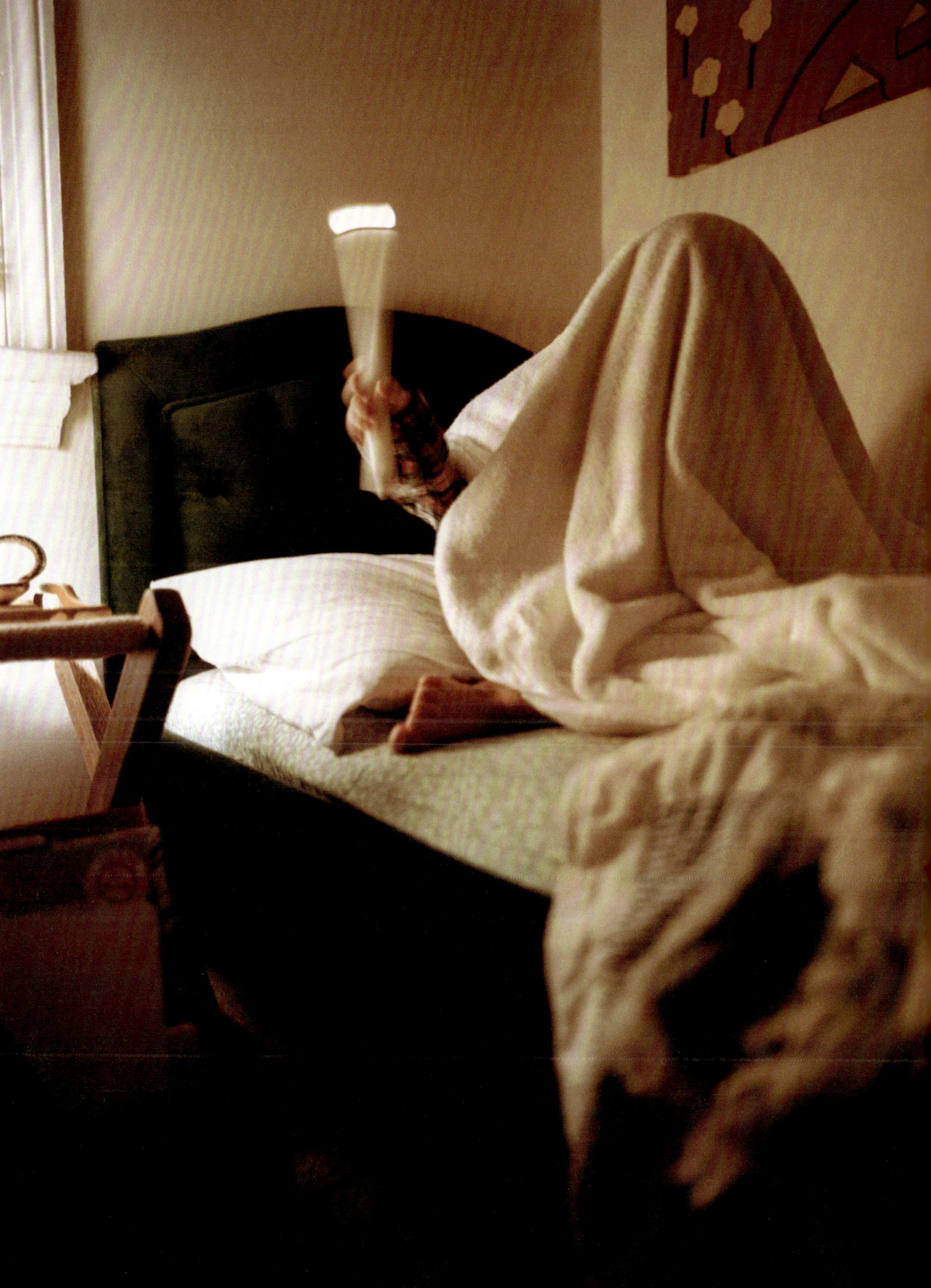

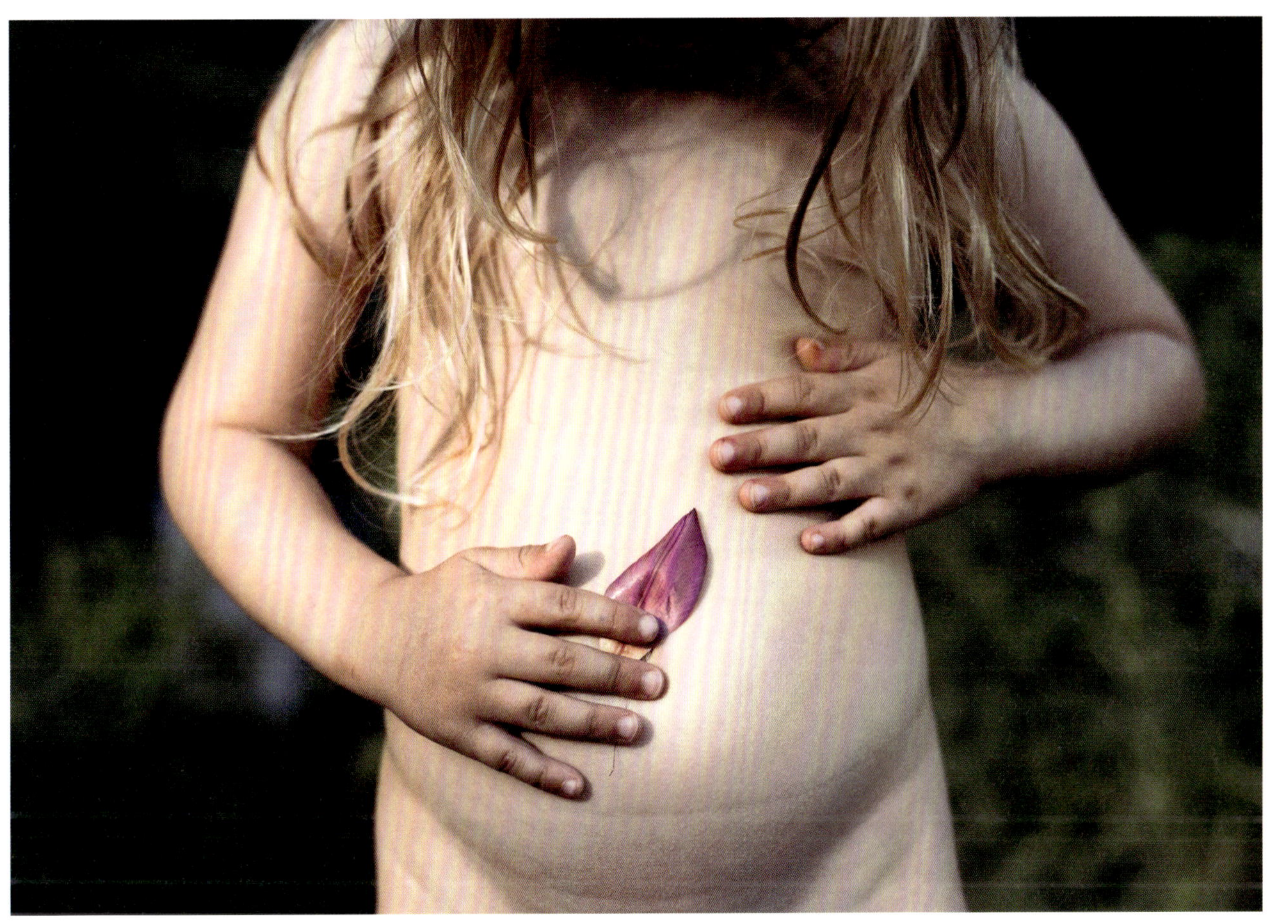

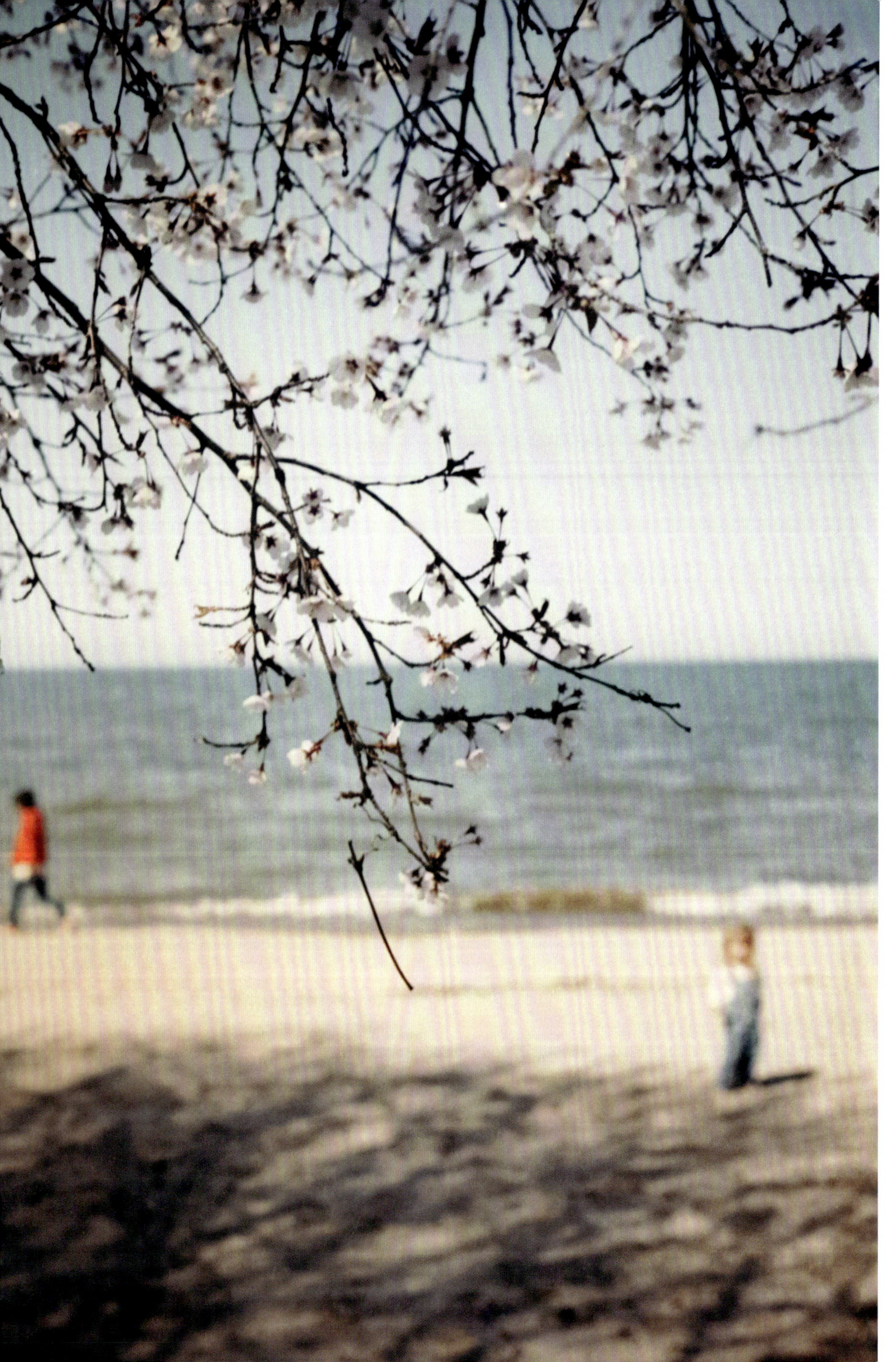

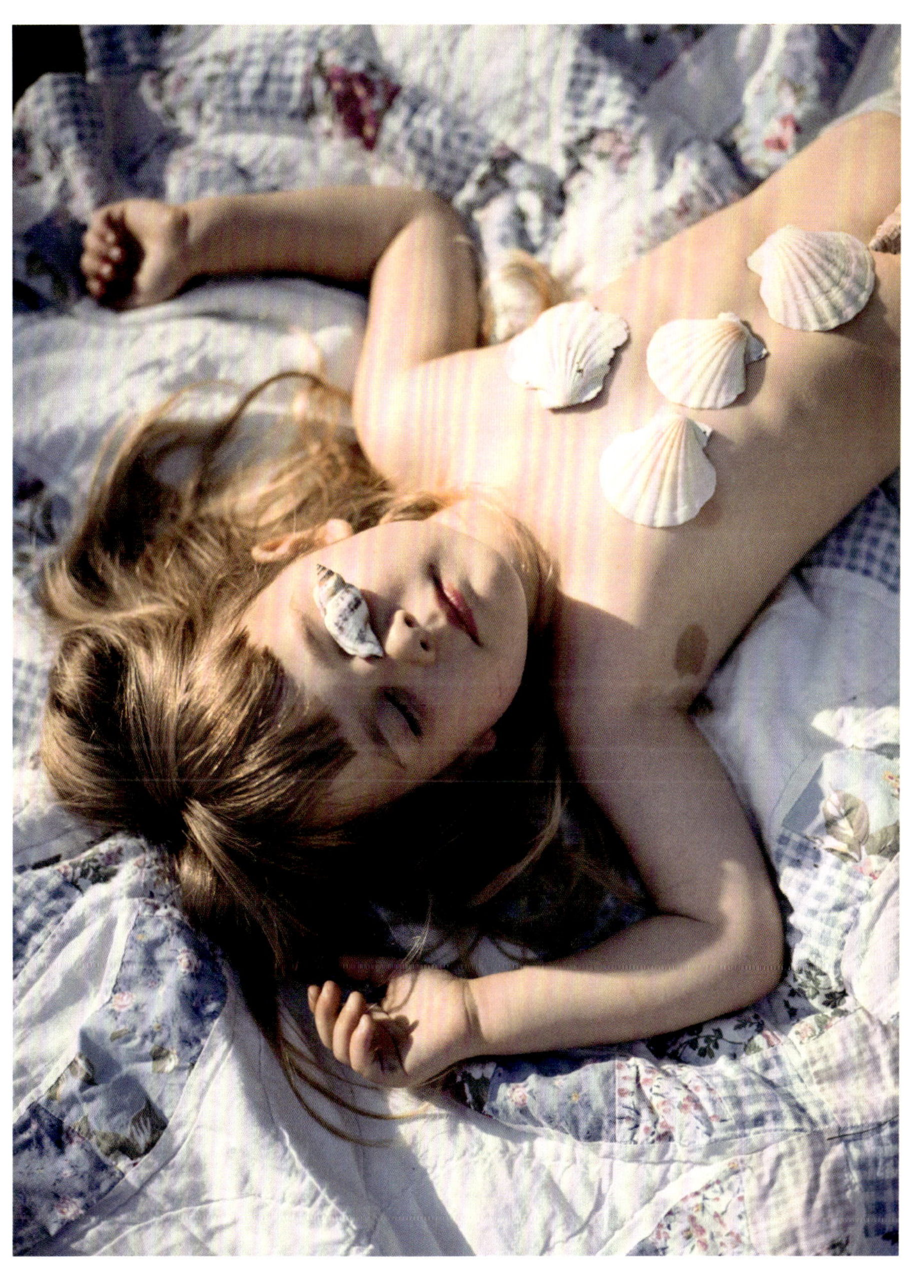

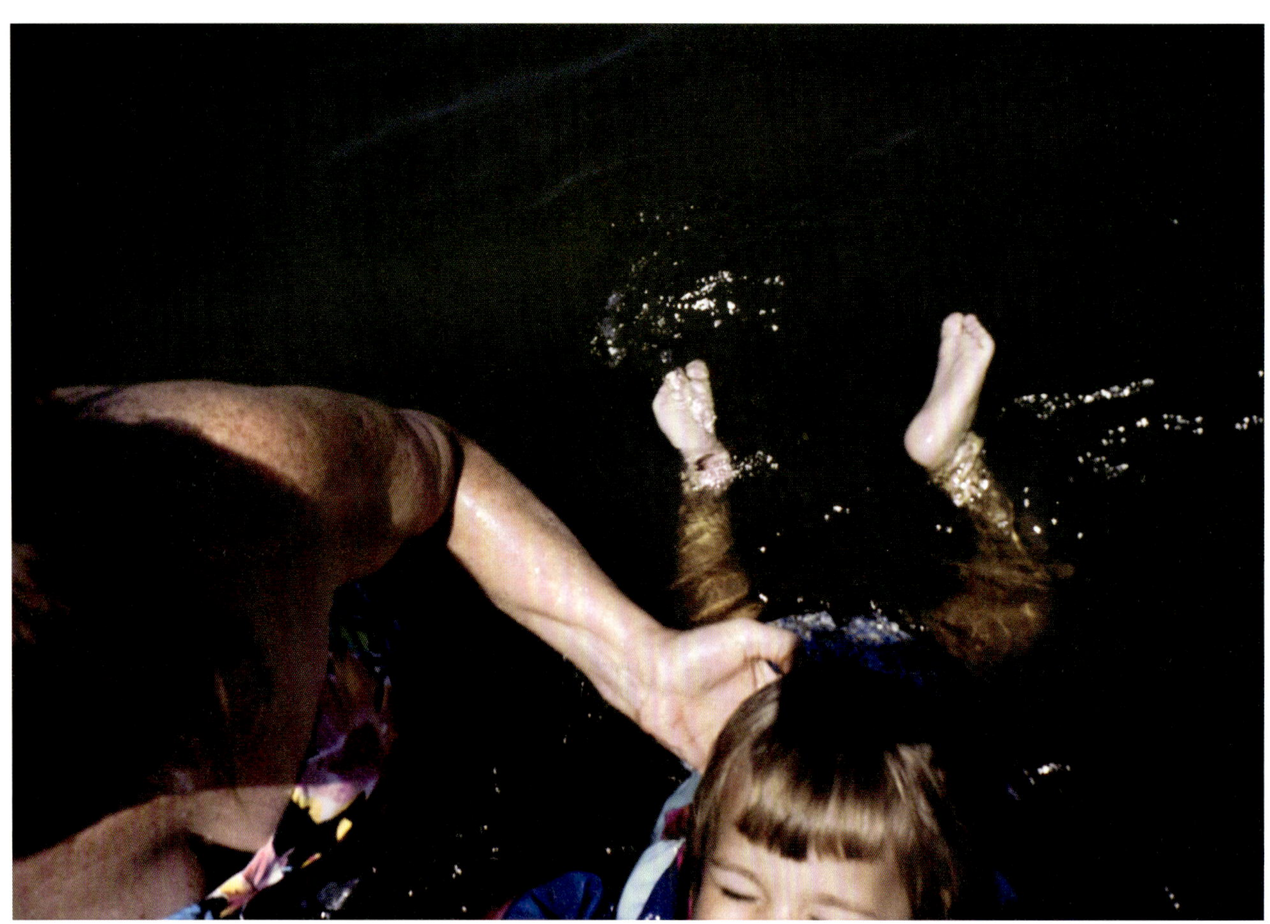

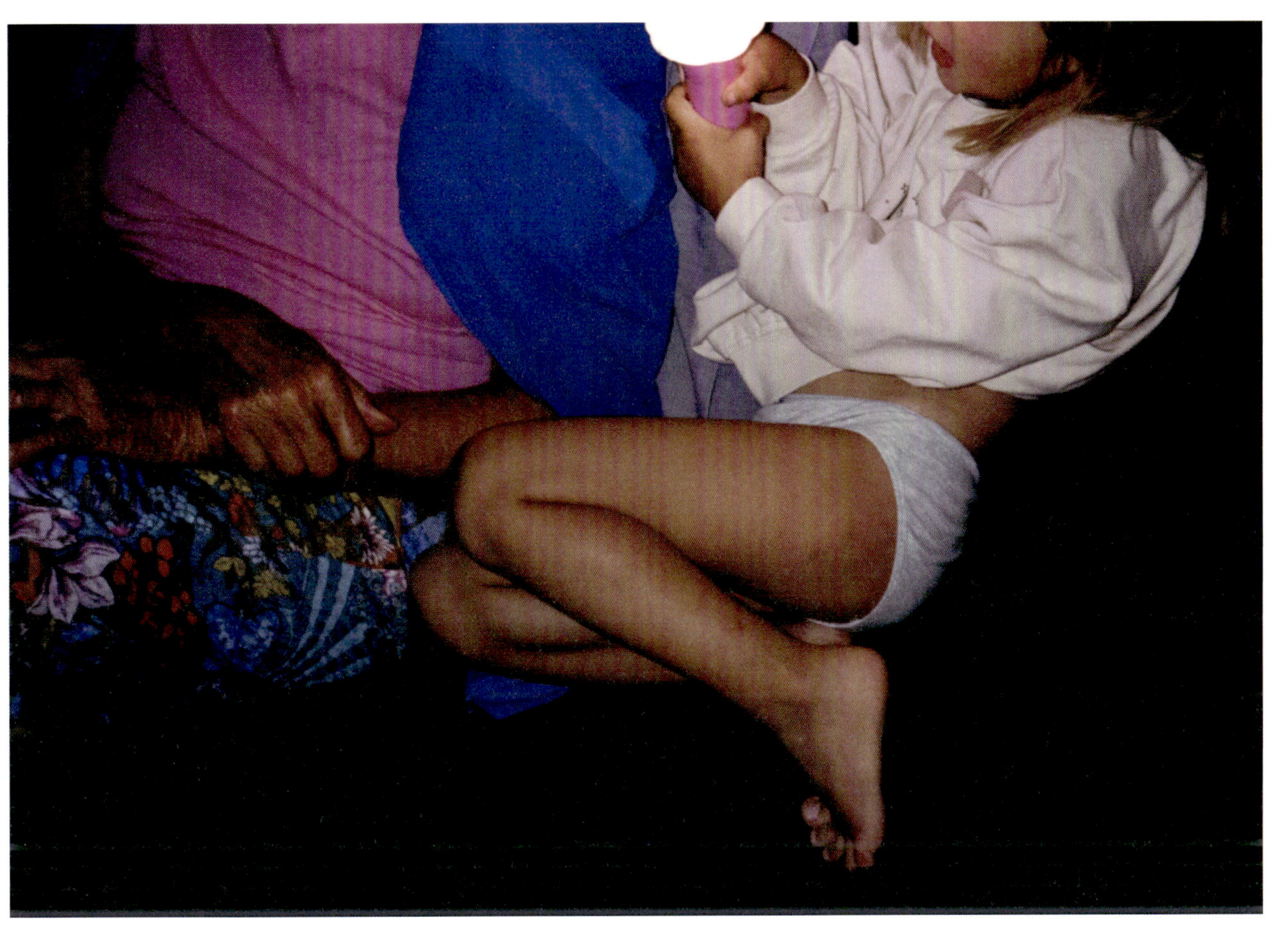

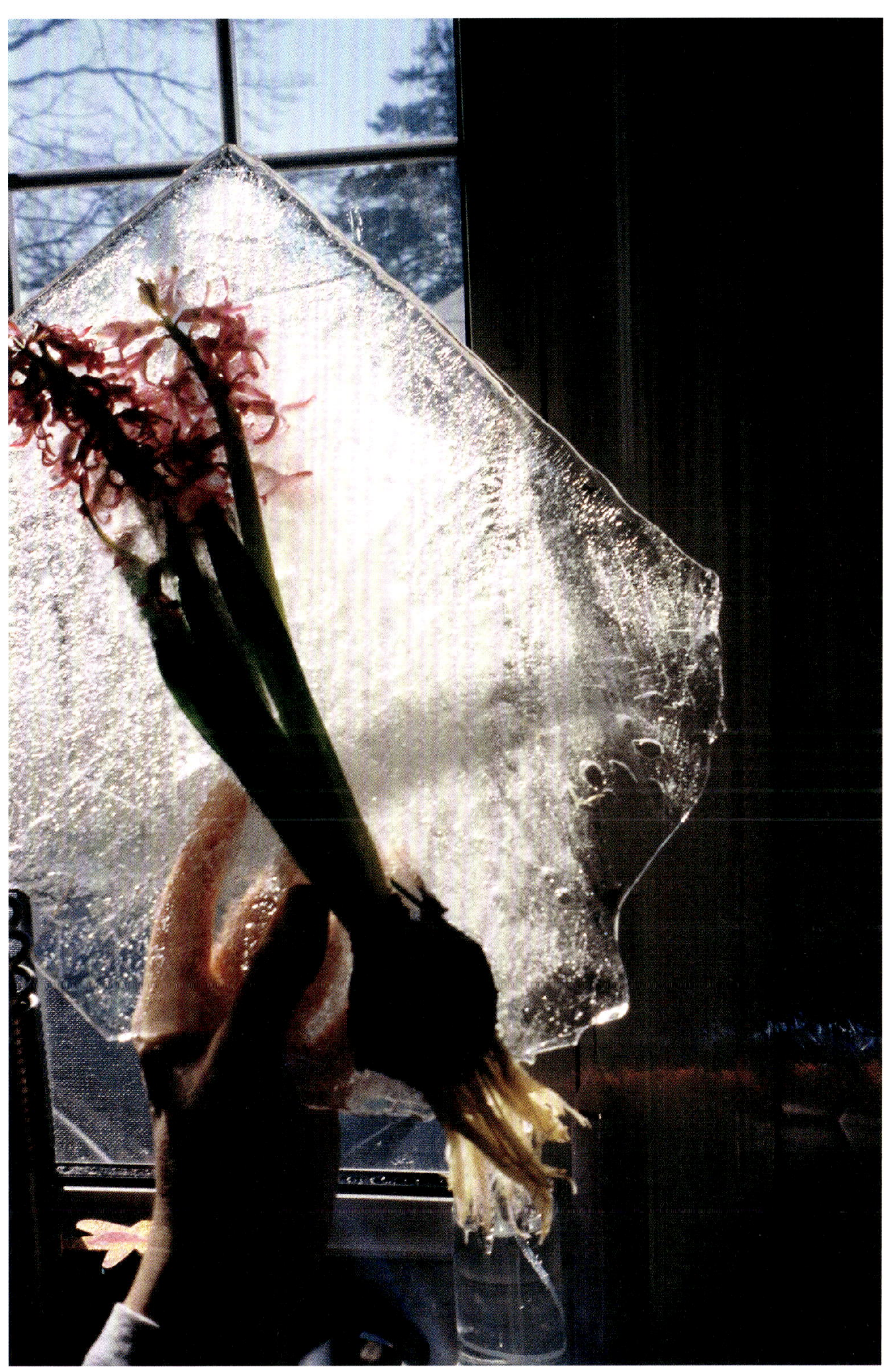

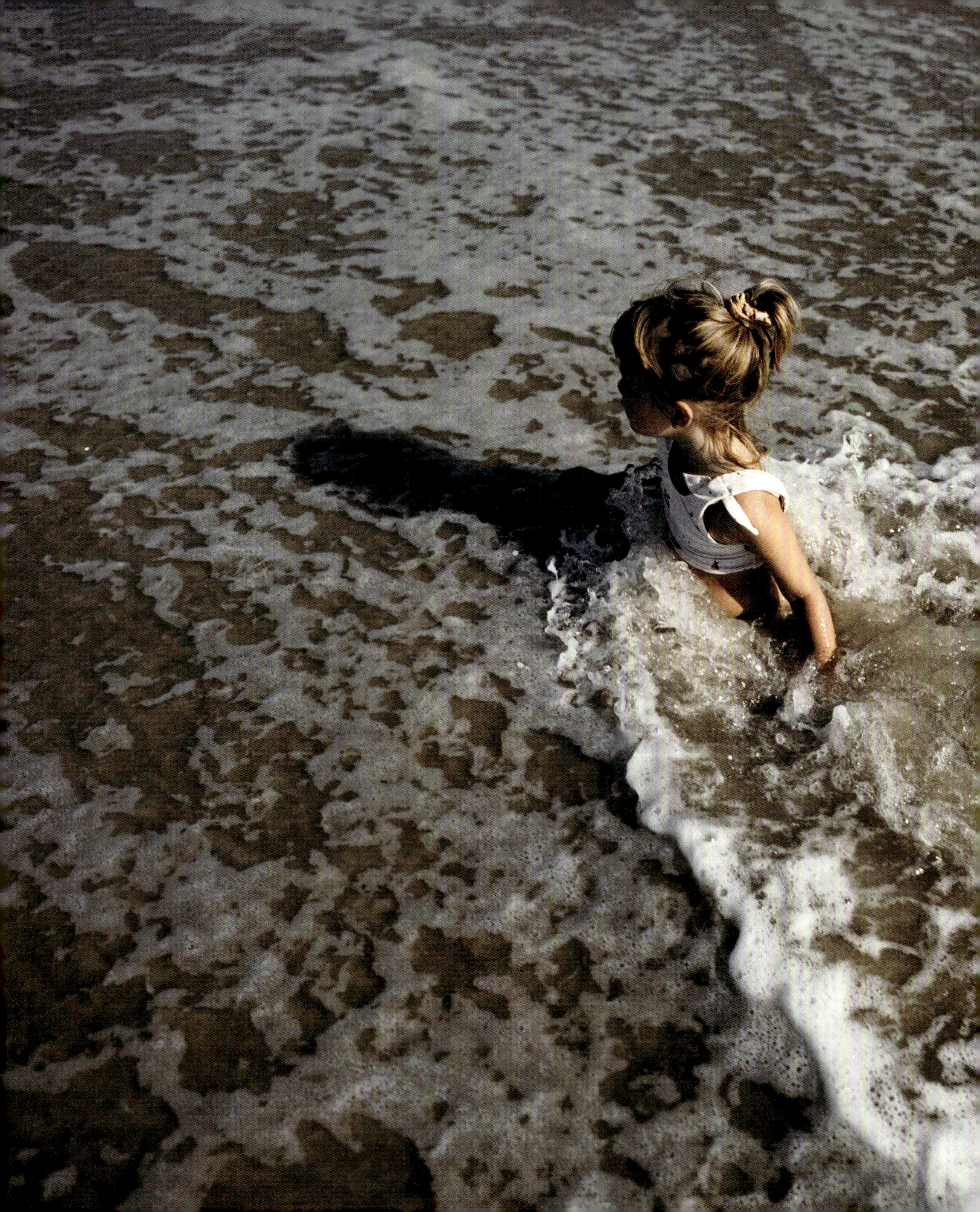

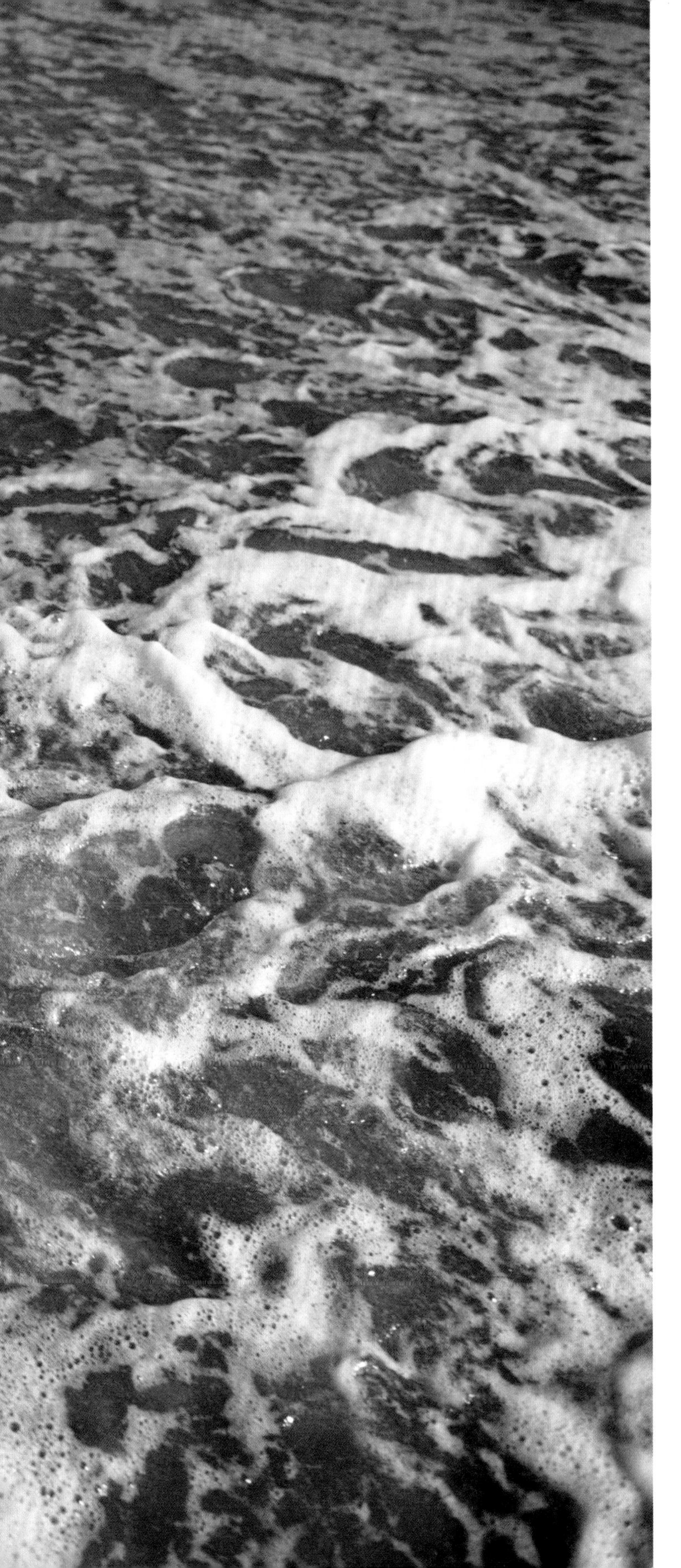

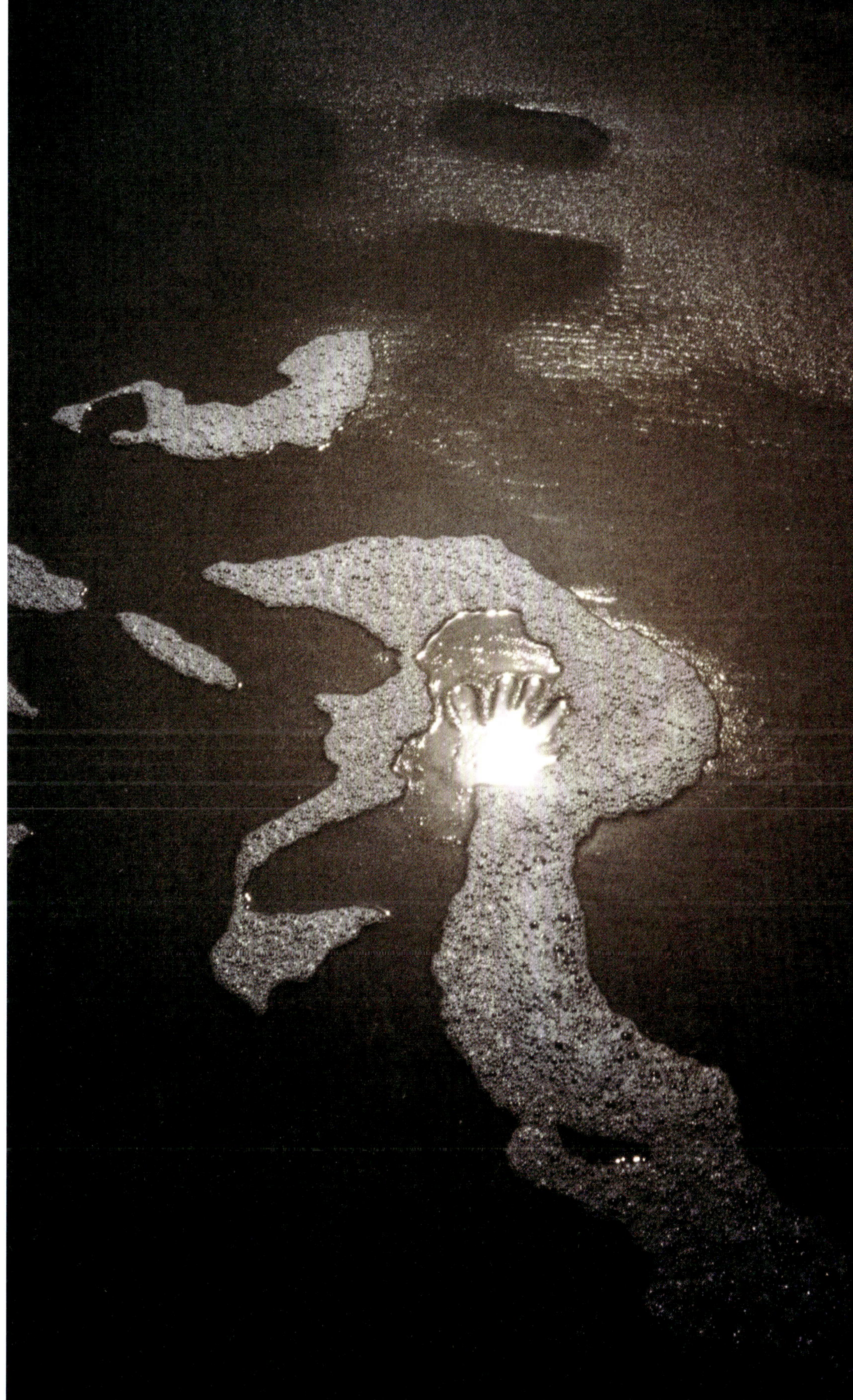

Grandlove

I first saw Jillian's series *We Keep Swimming, Until We All Reach Home* in the spring of 2023, and experienced a surprising feeling; it is okay, I felt, it is okay. I am fifty-two years old, a mother of two, and seeing Jillian's images gave me the feeling that it is okay: It is okay to get older, it is okay to be postmenopausal, to age, it is okay to look forward to being a grandmother, it is okay to want to be loved by my daughter-in-law. It is okay to hope.

It is okay to be a woman.

It is okay not to have to choose between motherhood and feminism or grandmotherhood and feminism, because they are not mutually exclusive.

One of the elements in Jillian's work that emphasizes this is the very intimate and close multigenerational images of her mother-in-law.

Growing up in the '70s and '80s, I was raised on the cultural cliché that was common at that time, of the tense, even hostile relationship women are destined to have with their mothers-in-law; words such as jealousy, pettiness, competitiveness, and even hatred were frequently used to describe this relationship. Then, when I was twenty-one, I started dating Eran, my future husband, and met his mother, Edna. She has been my mother-in-law for almost thirty years now, years that have taught me that those concepts are not preordained; in fact, a deep love has emerged over those years, in which we've shared good and bad times, seen each other's best and worst. She has cared for my children and me over the years, and occasionally mothered me. My son is nineteen years old now, and I was recently introduced to his girlfriend. I looked into her eyes, the eyes that loved my son, at her arms that hugged him, and I immediately loved her.

I have the privilege of still having my mother and mother-in-law in my life, of enjoying their wisdom and support. Seeing Edna and my mother become grandmothers was so inspiring to me, as a woman and as an artist.

Yet our society overlooks grandmotherhood. It romanticizes and even idealizes motherhood and its aesthetics, from "Madonna and Child" works of art to modern images of Princess Diana and her sons, and other famous mothers in their well-staged, flawless moments. Our society loves this censored version of motherhood, in which mothers are usually young women and in their fertile years. But it overlooks grandmotherhood, even though we know today from numerous studies that it is one of the most crucial elements in human development. Moreover, grandmothers tend to be women over forty-five or fifty, and our society often turns its gaze away from older women, missing so much about this rich time in women's lives; after years of domestic and professional responsibilities, these women can share their wisdom, experience, and beauty. Jillian chose to point her camera at this evolutionarily crucial, this beautiful and inspiring part of life, and move it to center stage.

But she first had to choose to welcome it into her own life—a choice many women face. In embracing the grandmother of one's children, both mother-in-law and daughter-in-law get a second, different chance to experience motherhood. The tremendous impact that becoming a mother has on women creates blood ties to a woman who was a stranger until she became a mother-in-law. She can become more: an ally, a mentor. In a counter-statement to what has often been perceived as a strained, complicated, and even negative secondary relationship, Jillian's work shows it to be a source of strength and empowerment, creating a more direct connection to her mother-in-law, perhaps even one that would make one's partner feel that he was an outsider in a sense. The experience of motherhood, as well as caring for the children, the grandchildren, creates a bond between the two women.

Becoming a mother also gives many women the opportunity to rediscover their own mothers, to witness them in older age as grandmothers to their children and to observe the changed aspects of their own personalities brought about by motherhood, allowing one's relationship with her mother to alter and evolve, develop and deepen.

Jillian let this primal maternal love, the first love we know as human beings, the love of a mother, grandmother, and mother-in-law, take the lead. Her mother and mother-in-law dominate her images, both as mothers and grandmothers, but also as the women that they are, with aspects of their personalities presented to the viewers. In one image, we see her mother-in-law, in a black bathing suit, looking toward the distant sky, projecting a fierce presence, strength; she is comfortable in her own skin, beautiful, strong, old, and inspiring. In another, we see her in a softer moment, surrendering to the sunlight, letting go, standing upright, strong yet vulnerable.

She is celebrating what our youth-obsessed culture may miss: the beauty of grandmothers. She echoes Mother

Nature, who gave women a few more years; women's life expectancy in the US is six years longer than men's, and according to some theories grandmotherhood is significant for the survival and flourishing of the next generation. And so we listen to nature in these photographs; Jillian connects this multigenerational relationship to nature. In her text, she talks of women carrying the egg from which their granddaughters will be made in their womb when carrying their children. In her work, we see the human connection juxtaposed with images of plants, flowers, trees, and landscapes.

Nature and motherhood are connected themes in the work of two photographers who studied the issues of motherhood intensely: Tierney Gearon (American, b. 1963) and Cheryle St. Onge (American, b. 1961). Like Guyette, Gearon shows in her work the multigenerational relationship between her, her mother, and her children and puts them in the context of environment and nature. She portrays her mother in different aspects of her life outside of motherhood and grandmotherhood, using color photography and natural light. In Cheryl St. Onge's work, which is in black and white, the setting of her mother's portraits is the farm where she and her mother lived together until her mother died from vascular dementia.

In these three bodies of work, the artists use a poetic title to enhance their viewers' understanding of it, a title that affects how their viewers read the images.

St. Onge's title, *Calling the Birds Home*, connects us to her mother's predementia life as a bird watcher and the themes of home and being called to come home, something we all remember done by our mothers, at times, throughout our lives. Gearon's *Daddy, where are you?* acknowledges the absence of the father or grandfather, thus emphasizing the responsibilities and burdens that mothers always carry and that fathers don't always. Guyette's *We Keep Swimming, Until We All Reach Home* describes an active situation that resonates with the action of motherhood and a need to function, never sink, always carry on, for herself and her offspring. With those poetic titles, viewers get into the work with a specific mindset and an indication as to what the artist is expressing, their voice.

Like Gearon and St. Onge, Jillian operates in an exclusive world of women; the men do not appear, and we are unaware of their existence. There is something ancient in this portrayal of traditions of women raising children among themselves. The Industrial Revolution of the late eighteenth and early nineteenth centuries changed the nature of work and mothering in Europe and other countries of the Western world. Working for a wage and, eventually, a salary became part of urban life, and childbirth and childcare, as a women-only area, started to change.

Jillian is using those feminine elements as symbols, as in the image in which she is braiding her mother's and daughter's hair into one braid, representing intergenerational connection and links between mother, daughter, and granddaughter, while she is woven in with her camera, connected by the action of photography. The camera is not only a way to connect, to discover, to see; it is also a justification to allow for more intergenerational experiences and situations to be performed, to happen.

With her camera, Guyette lets photography create this village we have forgotten, permitting the images to let motherhood be performed to one another. Becoming a mother forced her, like it does many mothers, into needing her mother and mother-in-law, required acceptance, collaboration, and bonds, and allowed for the discovery of one another. She now needs them, a necessity that is crucial for the bonds of family.

But she also needs them to make her work. Her art asks her to pay attention to her mother and mother-in-law through photography, giving them a stage and enhancing the "village."

This "village" is now gone from many modern lives. However, Jillian has managed to create it in her life and for her images, to inspire the viewers to let her images—of this ancient womanly magic, connection, and strength—take us back to the village, let it exist in our lives, and ask us to seek it, as she does.

—Elinor Carucci
February 2024

Again and again we try to remake the world.
My daughter grows from a wild strawberry
To a beating drum, centuries contained in
A single body. *Do you know, my love, how*
Much we've suffered? Outside my body,
She stands beside our personal histories
And yawns. God can only take so much.

—Kate Baer

Acknowledgments

This book is for you, Francesca. You teach me how to be a better mother, a better human, every single day.

I would like to extend all of my warmest gratitude to my mother and stepfather, my family and friends who have supported and encouraged me every step of the way.

To Mom, for always championing me. For allowing me to be unabashedly myself, and to test your comfort in a way that only a mother could.

To Robin, for letting me in with such generosity from day one. This book wouldn't exist without our relationship.

To Robert, for your unwavering support since we were mere children. The space you've allowed me over the years to wind my way towards this body of work is a gift. I am in awe of the faith you have in me.

To Jenn and Woody. Our unlikely childhood, our myriad of shared experience is ineffable. There is no greater gift to me than to have two people who understand, exactly.

To Alex, for always checking in, and always listening.

To Elinor, for your beautiful, thoughtfully written essay. Your encouragement breathed so much light into this work, and allowed it to flourish.

To Kate, the exact kind of woman I am honored to call a friend. There is no writing like yours that could so masterfully marry with these pictures.

To Lindsey, for being the sounding board that you are. I no longer feel like an island in a sea of scattered moms since you turned up.

To my original crit group: Patricia, Emily, Debbie, and Danna. Your early input was essential.

To Erica, for holding my hand during this entire process.

To Michael Itkoff of Daylight, for responding to these pictures with such sincerity. I may never have felt ready to share this work widely without it.

To Ursula Damm. I am eternally grateful for the energy you brought to the design of this book. You understood it so beautifully from the very beginning; it was the safest in your hands.

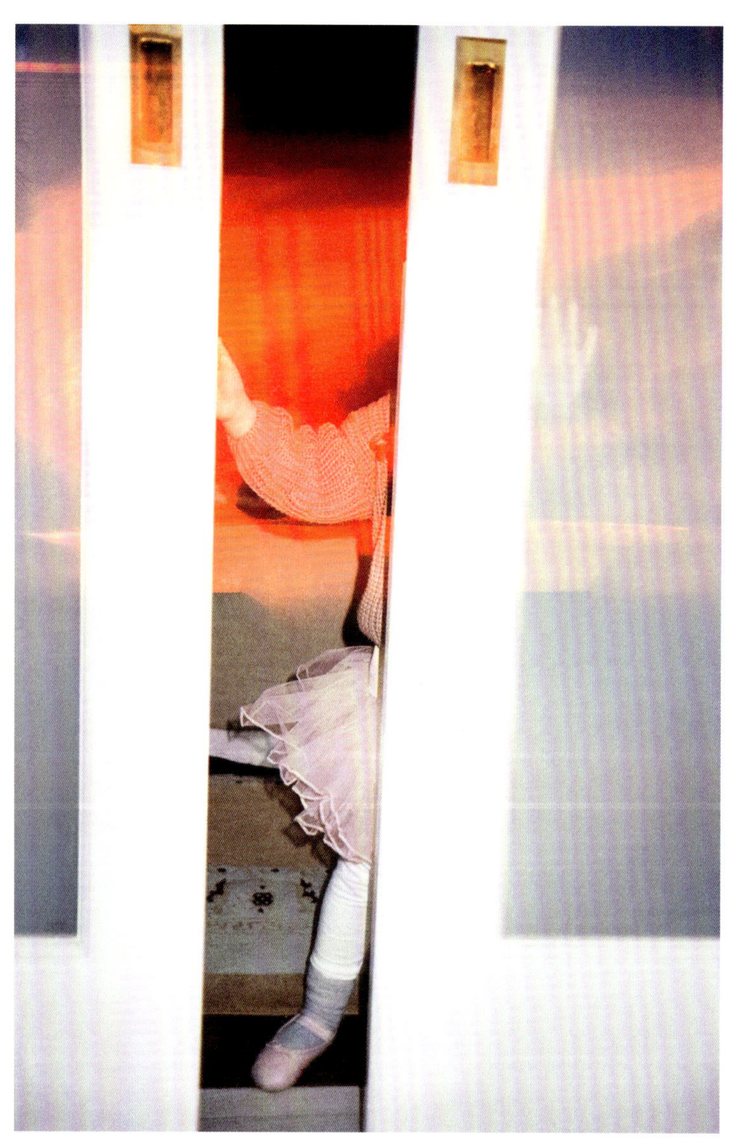